CHRIST OR THERAPY?

Christ or Therapy?
For Depression and Life's Troubles

E. S. Williams

THE WAKEMAN TRUST, LONDON
& BELMONT HOUSE PUBLISHING

CHRIST OR THERAPY?
© E. S. Williams, 2010

THE WAKEMAN TRUST & BELMONT HOUSE PUBLISHING
(Wakeman Trust is a UK Registered Charity)

Wakeman Trust UK Registered Office
38 Walcot Square
London SE11 4TZ

Wakeman Trust USA Office
300 Artino Drive
Oberlin, OH 44074-1263

Website: www.wakemantrust.org

Belmont House Publishing
36 The Crescent
Belmont
Sutton SM2 6BJ

Website: www.belmonthouse.co.uk

ISBN 978 1 870855 71 6

Cover design by Andrew Owen

Printed by Stephens & George, Merthyr Tydfil, UK

Contents

1
Christian Counselling – a Worldwide Movement

THE INFLUENCE of the Christian counselling movement is now ubiquitous in the Christian church, there being hardly any aspect of ministry that has not been touched in some way. It is widely accepted that psychological therapies, combined with Scripture, are needed for healing the emotional and behavioural problems that Christians experience. Seminars on depression, addressed by experts on the subject, are extremely popular, and Christian counsellors trained in the skills of psychotherapy, for a fee, provide a counselling ministry for the church. Many churches have arrangements to send anxious and depressed members of their congregations to counselling services.

Most theological colleges and seminaries have programmes on the theory and practice of counselling. Marriage enrichment programmes, which emphasise the importance of effective communication and conflict resolution, are spreading like wildfire across the Christian community in the UK, USA and other countries.

My earlier book on the subject, *The Dark Side of Christian Counselling* (2009), dealt with the growth of the Christian counselling movement in the USA and UK, and showed how the worldly wisdom of secular psychology has been combined with Scripture to help Christians suffering with emotional hurts and low self-esteem. The purpose of this book is to show how the flawed beliefs of the Christian counselling movement are affecting the doctrine and conduct of the church.

The beginnings of Christian counselling

A brief summary of the counselling movement's origins, set out fully in *The Dark Side,* is provided here for the help of readers. The Christian counselling movement developed in the USA after the Second World War when Christian psychologists claimed that believers suffering with emotional issues, like anxiety and depression, needed to be counselled by a trained psychotherapist. In the 1950s psychologist Clyde Narramore, widely regarded as the father of the Christian counselling movement, set up a mental health foundation that offered a version of counselling that combined secular psychological theories with Christian principles.

In the 1960s Fuller Theological Seminary established a School of Psychology to run alongside the School of Theology, and this rapidly became the intellectual powerhouse of the Christian counselling movement, offering a range of academic courses that sought to integrate psychological theory and Scripture. Christian psychologists were portrayed as possessing a special knowledge that enabled them to assist people on their journey to spiritual and emotional wholeness.

Christian counselling grew rapidly during the 1970s and 1980s as Christians, such as James Dobson, Larry Crabb, Gary Collins and Bruce Narramore, taught and authored books on the skills of psychotherapy. The American Association of Christian Counsellors (AACC), established in 1990, committed itself to the integration of biblical and psychological principles. The vision of this Association, which now claims to have over 50,000 members, is to serve the *worldwide* Christian church by training a large army of counsellors.

Christian counselling in the UK, under the inspiration of well-known writers such as Selwyn Hughes, has imported many ideas from the USA and also believes in combining psychological theories with Scripture. Leading proponents of counselling in the UK are CWR (Crusade for World Revival) and the London School of Theology. The Association of Christian Counsellors (ACC), established in 1992, claims to be the voice of Christian counselling in the UK. Its pastoral care foundation course 'aims to develop those with a heart for pastoral care, helping them be enabled to release the hands, feet and voice of Jesus into their local communities'.[1]

Integrating Scripture with psychological theories

Modern Christian counselling continues to be based on the combining of secular psychology with biblical teaching. It is claimed that the 'facts' of psychology are based on scientific truth, therefore psychological and biblical truth can be combined to produce 'all truth'. On the basis of this argument Christian counselling seeks to combine elements of Sigmund Freud's psychotherapy, Alfred Adler's goal-orientated counselling, Carl Rogers' client-centred counselling, Albert Ellis' rational emotive behavioural therapy (REBT), Abraham Maslow's needs-related psychology and Aaron Beck's cognitive therapy, into its armoury.

We are asked to accept that the psychological theories of men (indeed, men strongly opposed to Christianity and the teaching of the Bible) have acquired a standard of truth that allows them to stand alongside God's revealed Word. To achieve this integration Scripture is usually reinterpreted to fit psychological theory. The Bible is no longer the primary source of truth, but a secondary source used to support the latest psychological version of 'truth'. But Scripture teaches that God's words are Truth itself – they are the final standard and definition of Truth *(John 17.17; 18.37)*.

Another argument of the integrationists is that the Bible is good and well as far as it goes, but it is just not enough, for it does not deal adequately with the deep, complex issues people face today. This argument is based on the false idea that Scripture is not sufficient for dealing with profound behavioural problems. Yet the Bible declares the sufficiency of Christ, asserting that God has given to the believer in Christ 'all things that pertain to life and godliness' *(2 Peter 1.3)*. And God has blessed Christians 'with every spiritual blessing in the heavenly places in Christ' *(Ephesians 1.3)*. Christians are complete in Christ *(Colossians 2.10)* and do not need the wisdom of the world that flows from secular psychology. We don't need help from Freud and his friends to live a life worthy of the Gospel. The assertion that Christians need more than the Bible offers in order to face the problems of daily living is contrary to Scripture.

The giants of psychotherapy

The Dark Side of Christian Counselling has a chapter on each of the 'giants' of psychotherapy, namely Sigmund Freud, Alfred Adler, Abraham Maslow, Carl Rogers and Albert Ellis. Below is a brief summary.

Freud is the fountain-head of the psychotherapeutic movement. The unspoken motivation behind his work was a passion to subvert the Gospel of Christ. He had a fascination with the occult that undoubtedly influenced his model of psychotherapy. At the centre of Freud's model lies the unconscious mind, over which we have no control, that is the driving force of human behaviour. His sinister theory placed enormous power in the hands of the psychotherapist who alone can open the door to our unconscious mind, interpret its contents and deliver us from its tyranny. But the claim that a psychotherapist can delve into the unconscious mind is contrary to Scripture, for God alone knows the mind of man *(2 Chronicles 6.30)*.

Alfred Adler was a humanist who supported the godless philosophy of Nietzsche. His idea of a 'fictional' final goal, developed during childhood, has been used by Christian counsellors to understand human behaviour.

In Maslow's worldview, the problem with man, who is basically good, is that all his needs have not been met. He claimed that we need healthy self-esteem to feel significant and secure. Salvation is through psychotherapy which develops our human potential and takes us to the fount of self-actualisation. Maslow was hostile to the Gospel and his peak experiences involved New Age thinking.

Carl Rogers rejected all moral authority other than his own experience. Like Maslow, denying the biblical doctrine of original sin and human depravity, he believed that human nature is essentially healthy and has the potential for personal growth in a counselling situation. He taught that healthy self-esteem is essential for psychological health. His client-centred counselling model is non-directive, non-judgemental, and empathic. Clients must be helped to express and trust their feelings so that they can do what 'feels' to be right in a particular situation. Rogers' emphasis on feelings is contrary to Scripture for 'a fool vents all his feelings, but a wise man holds them back' *(Proverbs 29.11)*. His model is used by Christian counsellors to help a woman decide whether or not to have an abortion.

Ellis was a self-proclaimed atheist who despised devout Christians, referring to them as 'fanatical religionists'. In *The Case Against Religion* Ellis argues that 'if religion is defined as man's dependence on a power above and beyond the human, then, as a psychotherapist, I find it to be exceptionally pernicious.'[2] All true believers 'are distinctly disturbed, since they are obviously rigid, fanatic and dependent individuals.'[3] In his view committed Christians are suffering with a form of mental illness. His rational emotive behaviour therapy helps Christians to change their core beliefs in order to behave in a more rational way.

The teachings of these giants of psychology are, according to Scripture, pure folly, for they disregard the spiritual dimension of life, deny the doctrine of original sin and reject the moral law of God. It is not difficult to see that the psychological speculations of these men are *fundamentally* opposed to the most basic doctrines of the Christian faith. Scripture says that unbelievers are darkened in their understanding, being alienated from the life of God because of the ignorance that is in them, due to the hardness of their heart *(Ephesians 4.18)*. The common ground between these five men is that they were unbelievers who, in their lives and theories, rejected the God of Scripture. The god of this world had blinded their minds *(2 Corinthians 4.4)*. But their theories are the foundation and pillars of 'psychological truth'. The Christian counselling movement is integrating into the church of Christ the psychological speculations that have come from the futile thinking of these godless men.

Scripture teaches that the problem of human behaviour lies in the heart of man – out of the heart comes all manner of sinful conduct, from sexual immorality, to deceit, theft, covetousness, pride and murder *(Mark 7.20-23)*.

Why have the giants of psychology got it so wrong? The answer is – because their psychological theories are the product of minds darkened by unbelief. Their worldly wisdom is foolishness in God's sight. Can their foolish 'wisdom' lead the church into yet more truth? No, for all the treasures of wisdom and knowledge are hid in Christ *(Colossians 2.3)*. And no again, for the Spirit of Truth 'will guide you into *all* truth' *(John 16.13)*.

The disaster of integrating psychotherapy and Scripture is that it has mixed God's Truth with ungodly ideas. The integrationists' passion for the foolish theories of psychotherapy shows that they are striving to serve two masters. Their heart is divided between Christ and the giants of psychotherapy, and they love their psychotherapeutic techniques more than they love the Word of God. They are not satisfied with God's provision; they seek to supplement God's Word with the wisdom of the world. They want to have communion with the dark teachings of the giants of psychology. But Scripture makes it clear that Christians are not to be yoked together with unbelievers. For what communion has light with darkness *(2 Corinthians 6.14)*?

The true church will have nothing to do with the foolishness of the giants of psychotherapy. It is unthinkable that such teachings can be integrated with God's Word. Those who do so are either being deceived by the false philosophy of this world *(Colossians 2.8)*, or they are false teachers who are deliberately introducing destructive heresy into the church *(Jude 4)*.

A worldwide movement

The Christian counselling movement has spread its tentacles worldwide, and there is hardly a country on earth that is not in its grip. Fuller Seminary's School of Psychology has developed a programme to equip Christian counsellors by making 'resources available free of charge to seminaries, Bible schools, and Christian counselling agencies in Africa who will be able to utilise them in the training of counsellors'.[4] The book *Christian Counselling: an African Indigenous Perspective* (2006), written by a Kenyan graduate of Fuller, is used in seminars to teach the principles of Christian counselling in an African context. As a result of Fuller's pervasive influence, the psychological way is rapidly engulfing African churches. The Kenyan-based Oasis Counselling Centre believes that the importance of counselling in the church cannot be over-emphasised and is preparing training materials and running seminars throughout Africa to prepare Christian counsellors.[5]

The Association of Christian Counsellors of Nigeria was set up in

2008, based on the model of the AACC, with the aim of administering holistic Christian counselling. The president of the new association issued this challenge: 'Can we come together and make our national association [do] what the American Association has done for America and mankind? Of course we can, if Christian professionals from different fields, ministers and Christian counsellors, teachers and trained counsellors who practise as Christian counsellors could sign up membership . . .'[6]

The psychological way of thinking has penetrated many missionary agencies. Dr Ron Koteskey, a consultant psychologist for GO International, explains that psychological tests are used with missionaries for many purposes. 'Some tests may be used in the selection process to screen out people from being missionaries. Others are used to help place people in the positions where they will be most effective. Others are used to give missionaries insights into their own personality traits and the traits of others with whom they work so that they can better work together.' He says that the Myers-Briggs Type Indicator, developed from Carl Jung's personality theory, is widely used within mission agencies 'to help people understand themselves and others along four dimensions, such as introversion-extraversion'. He sums up the benefits: 'Psychological tests are not given to harm people, but to help them. Gaining insight into yourself and being placed in the right position in the organisation leads to personal growth and to more effective work in the kingdom.'[7] It is no surprise, then, that the counselling ethos has found a home in missionary societies.

What is happening in Africa is also happening in other developing nations. Fuller has established a relationship with Chinese seminaries, psychological institutes and universities with the aim of supporting the growing church in China in the critical areas of pastoral counselling. Fuller has been awarded a large grant from the John Templeton Foundation, an organisation with a strong New Age ethos (see chapter 6), for a project to advance the scholarship of psychology, science, and religion in Chinese society. The project aims to create a Chinese Association of Psychologists of Religion and to build on existing partnerships between select Chinese universities and Fuller's School of Psychology.[8]

Such is the joint commitment of Fuller's Seminary and the AACC to go into all the world and preach a psychotherapeutic gospel, that in 2005 the International Network for Christian Counselling (INCC) was set up. Its mission is to promote counselling worldwide by the dissemination of information, educational resources and counselling aids. The network plans to help with the establishment of national counselling associations in countries around the world. On the board of trustees is Dr Archibald Hart, Professor of Psychology at Fuller's.

The Lausanne movement

The Lausanne movement for world evangelism, set up in 1974 by Billy Graham, John Stott and other 'pillars' of much of evangelicalism, has become convinced that preaching the whole Gospel, to the whole world, means bringing inner healing through psychotherapy. To this end, in 2007 the Lausanne Committee invited psychologist Dr Brad Smith to become the coordinator of Care and Counsel International (CCI), an organisation 'that brings biblically grounded, psychologically sound, and culturally appropriate care and counsel to individuals and groups worldwide'.[9]

According to Brad Smith: 'God appears to have been growing a diverse group of Christ-followers who bring wisdom, compassion, and specialised skills to people who suffer from emotional and spiritual brokenness. The work of these helpers is called counselling, pastoral care, spiritual direction, psychotherapy, coaching, mentoring, social work, crisis intervention, trauma treatment and more. Their numbers include highly skilled, professionally trained psychiatrists, psychologists, social workers, pastoral counsellors, and others who seek to be competent practitioners committed to the highest ethical standards.' In the eyes of the Lausanne Committee the whole Gospel includes a psychotherapeutic message delivered by Christian counsellors that brings emotional healing. They see a great need for more Christian counselling and psychology to serve the poor in Jesus' name.[10]

Doctrine and conduct distorted

The objective of this book is to show how the flawed beliefs of the Christian counselling movement are affecting both the doctrine and conduct of the church. First we shall look at depression, a major issue facing society and the church. The counselling movement spends much of its time and receives most of its income for providing psychotherapy to Christians suffering with depression. We need to understand what the Bible teaches about depression.

Then we shall take a look at the new concept of *unconditional love* that is widely accepted in the church. Another big issue is that of forgiveness, as many Christians believe that they are required to forgive all who offend against them no matter what. But what is the biblical view of forgiveness? Marriage education has become popular among churches as many seek to understand the recipe for a long-lasting successful relationship. Do Christians need the psychological techniques of effective communication, reflective listening and conflict resolution to have a successful marriage?

While some Christians are becoming uneasy about the counselling scene, few are inclined to raise the alarm, feeling that counselling is a secondary issue, the primary issue being to preach the Gospel. However, this entirely misses the point for, as we shall see in this book, the psychological infiltration of the church is actually changing the Gospel of Truth. The Gospel is being increasingly distorted and therefore true salvation is being denied to a generation. Those who would fight the good fight of faith must contend for the Gospel of Truth once for all delivered to the saints and oppose the seductive theories of the Christian counselling movement.

2
The Psycho-Secular Model of Depression

A FLOOD OF DEPRESSION, or so it seems, is now over-whelming both the church and society as a whole. According to the World Health Organisation clinical depression is currently a leading cause of disability in the USA and UK and other Western nations. Psychiatrists see more people suffering from depression than from all other emotional problems put together. In the UK depression and anxiety are now the most common reasons for people submitting claims for long-term sickness benefits. Such is the size of the problem that over 30 million prescriptions for antidepressants are issued each year.

To deal with the growing number of depressed Christians many churches are now organising seminars to give church leaders and congregations advice on how to deal with the problem. Some pastors consider the issue to be so important that they encourage the entire congregation to attend a depression seminar.

Church-based depression seminars, usually given by Christians with experience in counselling, emphasise two things. The first is that

Christians suffer with depression just like everybody else. A number of Scriptures are quoted to support this view, usually including the 'depression' of Elijah, Job and Jeremiah, and numerous texts from the *Psalms*. The second point is that clinical depression is an established disease just like diabetes or cancer. Therefore a Christian suffering from clinical depression is mentally ill and needs to be treated. Those who hold to this view of depression say that the last thing clinically depressed people need is to have biblical texts quoted at them, as this is likely to aggravate their condition. The accepted treatment for depression includes both suitable counselling and antidepressants.

The burden of depression among Christians can be judged by the large number of books on the subject that are currently available from the local Christian bookshop. A search of the Wesley Owen website produced 93 titles, which included the following: *How to Win over Depression*; *Depression – A Rescue Plan*; *Hope in the Midst of Depression*; *Pathways Through Depression*; *100 Ways to Overcome Depression*; *Overcoming Depression*; *Seeing Beyond Depression*; *New Light on Depression*; *Victory Over Depression*; *Finding Your Way Through Depression*; *Discouragement and Depression*; *Comfort for Depression*; *Living with Depression*; *Coping with Depression,* and many more similar titles.

In *A Practical Workbook for the Depressed Christian* (1991) Dr John Lockley, a British general practitioner, shares his passionate conviction that for Christians depression rarely has a spiritual cause. His central theme is that depression is an illness and that great good would come if ignorance and prejudice were replaced with facts and sympathy. Dr Lockley claims that it is usually impossible to snap out of depression or find instant healing. He believes that the church often makes it worse by heaping guilt on sufferers and telling them that learning to cope with depression can be a spiritual gymnasium through which God makes us more fitted to carry out his plans. His book promotes psychotherapy as helpful in treating depression.

What does the term 'depression' mean?

The purpose of this chapter is to describe the model of depression that has been developed by the world of psychiatry, before considering a biblical response in the next chapter. We need to understand what is actually meant by the term 'depression' as used by the mental health profession. How do we know the difference between a mental illness called depression, and *normal* feelings of sadness, despair or misery? The answer to this question is complicated by the fact that the word 'depression' is now commonly used to express the way we feel when things go against us. We feel depressed when a relationship breaks up, when we have an argument with our spouse, when our football team is beaten, when we lose a job, or at the death of a family member or close friend. So what emotions, feelings, conditions or disorders qualify as a mental illness 'depression', and what feelings and emotions are simply a part of normal everyday life that all people experience from time to time? In other words, when do our feelings of 'depression' constitute a mental illness?

Defining depression

The concept of 'depression' that has emerged from the world of psychiatry (spurred on by the pharmaceutical industry) is not as clear cut as many people believe. Fifty years ago, when I was a medical student, recognisable clinical depression was a relatively rare condition. In the first part of the 20th century only two syndromes involving depression were mentioned in psychiatric text books, the depressive phase of manic depression and severe depression in old age known as involutional melancholia. When the first antidepressant was developed in the 1950s, the drug manufacturer Geigy was reluctant to market it, judging that there were not enough people with depression to make the drug profitable.[1]

But times have changed and the last four decades have been characterised by an escalating interest in the subject of depression, driven by the growth in psychiatry and psychological counselling, and the development of an increasing number of antidepressant drugs. The result is that more and more people have been labelled as depressed and large numbers are being prescribed drugs to alleviate their symptoms.

'The Diagnostic and Statistical Manual of Mental Disorders (DSM)'

The diagnostic criteria for depression are laid down by the *Diagnostic and Statistical Manual of Mental Disorders (DSM)* of the American

Psychiatric Association. The first edition *(DSM-I)*, published in 1952, classified depression as a psychosis, either involutional melancholia or manic-depressive psychosis, which included endogenous (that is, no known cause) depression. Under this regime depression was a relatively rare event.

The third edition of the *Diagnostic Manual of Mental Disorders (DSM-III)*, published in 1980, created an entirely new way of looking at depression by introducing a descriptive symptom-based approach to mental illness. Dr Robert Spitzer, a psychiatrist who identified himself as an atheist and a secular humanist,[2] was the driving force behind *DSM-III*. It was his energy and commitment (that defined more than a hundred mental disorders) that revolutionised the practice of psychiatry. Where there had been a few psychiatric diseases, such as schizophrenia, there were now a host of 'disorders'. Spitzer's skill was his ability to describe each new mental disorder and to create a checklist of symptoms that were needed to justify a diagnosis.

So the list of symptoms for establishing a diagnosis of clinical depression was constructed by Robert Spitzer, taking into account the opinions of American mental health specialists. This means that the diagnostic criteria for depression have been created by the subjective opinions of psychiatrists and psychological counsellors, and not on any objective scientific evidence. Henceforth depression would be diagnosed by a long list of symptoms created by the majority opinion of psychiatrists, the very profession that stood to profit from increasing the number of depressed people in society.

The fourth edition of the *Diagnostic Manual (DSM-IV)*, published in 1994, gives a profoundly subjective and arbitrary definition of depression. There are three requirements – the first is that at least five symptoms need to be present; the second is that these symptoms must be present during the same two-week period; the third is that these symptoms must represent a change from a previous level of functioning.

A brochure produced by the American Psychiatric Association informs the reader that 'depression is a *serious medical illness* that negatively affects how you *feel,* the way you *think* and how you *act.* Depression has a variety of symptoms, but the [two] most common are a deep feeling of sadness or a marked loss of interest or pleasure in activities. Other symptoms include: changes in appetite that result in weight losses or gains unrelated to dieting, insomnia or oversleeping, loss of energy or increased fatigue, restlessness or irritability, feelings of worthlessness or inappropriate guilt, difficulty thinking, concentrating, or making decisions and thoughts of death or suicide or attempts at suicide.'

'Depression is common. It affects nearly one in 10 adults each year – nearly twice as many women as men. It's also important to note that depression can strike at any time, but on average, first appears during the late teens to mid-20s. Depression is also common in older adults. Fortunately, depression is very treatable.'[3]

Note that in the eyes of the Association, depression is an *illness* that affects our feelings, thinking and actions. It follows that people suffering from depression, *a serious medical illness*, cannot necessarily be held responsible for the way they feel, think or act.

According to the National Institute of Mental Health there is no single known cause of depression. 'Rather, it likely results from a combination of genetic, biochemical, environmental, and psychological factors. Research indicates that *depressive illnesses are disorders of the brain* . . . The parts of the brain responsible for regulating mood, thinking, sleep, appetite and behaviour appear to function abnormally. In addition, important neurotransmitters – chemicals that brain cells use to communicate – appear to be out of balance.'[4]

So while the exact cause of depression is not known, the mental health profession claims that depression is due to abnormal brain function caused by an imbalance of brain chemicals. Once again we are told that depression is a disorder of the brain that affects our thinking and behaviour.

Note the highly subjective nature of the diagnosis, for it depends entirely on what the patient tells the psychiatrist or counsellor, and they have no way of knowing if the patient is reporting matters accurately. The psychiatrist or counsellor must use his clinical judgement to decide whether the patient's self-reported symptoms fulfil the diagnostic criteria to earn the label of clinical depression. The diagnostic difficulties are easy to see. How many people suffer, from time to time, with fatigue, insomnia, indecisiveness or diminished interest in pleasures? And how does the clinician know that patients' self-reported symptoms are a new phenomenon in their lives? And there is another major problem. Many people stand to benefit from a diagnosis of clinical depression, for they are then considered to be sick and therefore not responsible for their behaviour. They may also be able to take time off work and even claim disability benefits. In addition, the clinician stands to benefit financially by confirming a diagnosis of depression for he now has a patient to treat. (Notice the reassurance of the American Psychiatric Association that depression is very treatable.)

Another diagnostic difficulty is that clinicians vary in the way they interpret a patient's symptoms. Take the symptom 'feelings of inappropriate guilt'. How does a clinician distinguish between appropriate and inappropriate guilt? Indeed, what one clinician diagnoses as 'inappropriate guilt' may be regarded very differently by another.

What all this means is that the diagnosis of depression is highly arbitrary and totally subjective. We must underline the fact that there are no clear, objective or truly measurable diagnostic criteria. There is no physical sign, blood test or X-Ray that can confirm the diagnosis. All depends on what the patient says and how the psychiatrist or counsellor interprets it.

To distinguish between mood changes that all people experience as a part of the give and take of life, and 'clinical' depression is a very difficult task. And we must remember that to make a diagnosis of clinical depression might serve the interests of both the patient and the clinician.

In his essay 'Don't be happy, worry', book reviewer Jerome Weeks argues that a consequence 'of defining depression downward has been an inability to distinguish – with any accuracy – severe depression from garden-variety glumness. Drug companies and doctors started a cascade, a blurring of categories between depression and anxiety, anger, laziness or low self-esteem. Treating them represented a huge market expansion into "lifestyle issues". As a result, millions of people have been prescribed pills – that is, treated as if they were ill – when they were just feeling, well, sad.'[5] Weeks is simply emphasising the vagueness of the depression concept and pointing to the vested interests that stand to gain from increasing the number of depressed people in society.

Professor of Psychiatry Gordon Parker, in an article in the *British Medical Journal*, argues that depression is being hopelessly over diagnosed. He gives as an example a study of 242 teachers. Over time, ninety-five per cent reported symptoms and feelings that were consistent with a diagnosis of depression. Parker argues that a low threshold for diagnosing clinical depression risks treating normal emotional states as illness.[6] Indeed, if ten per cent of the population suffers with depression (*a serious medical illness*) each year, as we are informed by the American Psychiatric Association, over time almost the entire population will have suffered with *a serious disorder of the brain.*

The above discussion shows how the broad, inclusive concept of depression in the *DSM* has opened the depression floodgate. So how reliable is its definition of clinical depression? Here we need to recognise that the *DSM* is strongly influenced by the large pharmaceutical companies that produce antidepressants. A research study into the link between *DSM* panel members and pharmaceutical companies found that more than half had financial associations with the pharmaceutical industry.[7] Dr Lisa Cosgrove, a clinical psychologist, said that such research 'demonstrates that there are strong financial ties between the industry and those who are responsible for developing and modifying the diagnostic criteria for mental illness. The connections are especially strong in those diagnostic areas where drugs are the first line of treatment for mental disorders.' Dr Cosgrove made the point that 'pharmaceutical companies have a vested interest in what mental disorders are included in the *DSM*. Therefore, the most obvious implication is that "BigPharma" is influencing the inclusion of new disorders and/ or influencing the expansion of symptomatology.'

Dr Cosgrove further argues that 'transparency is especially important when there are multiple and continuous financial relationships between panel members and the pharmaceutical industry, because of the greater likelihood that *the drug industry may be exerting an undue influence on the DSM.* For example, the *DSM* working groups that had the highest percentage of financial ties to the pharmaceutical industry were those groups working in diagnostic areas (eg: mood disorders and psychotic disorders) where pharmacological interventions are standard treatment. In light of the extreme profitability of the psychotropic drug market, the connections found in this study between the *DSM* and the pharmaceutical industry are cause for concern.'[8] (My italics.)

This is a crucially important point to understand. The subjective criteria used for making a diagnosis of depression have been established by clinicians (psychiatrists and psychotherapists) who have a link to the pharmaceutical industry. By broadening the diagnostic criteria, the *DSM* has helped create a large market for psychotherapy and anti-depressant drugs.

'DSM' rooted in secular humanism

Here we must also emphasise that the model of depression constructed by secular humanist Dr Robert Spitzer is based on the tenets of secular humanism. Dr Ed Payne, editor of the *Journal of Biblical Ethics in Medicine*, makes the point that psychiatry, and thus the *DSM-IV*, is rooted in secular humanism. 'Sigmund Freud, Carl Jung, and other "fathers" were often avowed atheists. Their modern counterparts have continued this separation of religion, specifically biblical Christianity, from psychiatry. A Christian with any understanding of spiritual issues should ask, "How can an understanding of the thinking and behaviour of man omit the record and explanations of him who created, cursed, and saved mankind?" Any basic understanding of Christianity and philosophy reveals the incompatibility of concepts that grow out of secular humanism and biblical truth. The war of these worldviews is seen in every area of society – sexual norms, alcoholism, addiction, marriage, child-rearing, abortion, euthanasia, in vitro fertilisation, gun control, etc.'[9] Dr Payne is drawing attention to the ideology that underpins the *DSM* – secular humanism.

Two new mental disorders created by *DSM-IV* – 'conduct disorder' and 'oppositional defiant disorder' – illustrate the secular, godless mindset that drives the world of psychiatry. Children and adolescents with 'conduct disorder', according to *DSM-IV*, 'may display bullying, threatening, or intimidating behaviour; initiate frequent physical fights; use a weapon that can cause serious physical harm (eg: a bat, brick, broken bottle, knife, or gun); be physically cruel to people or animals; steal while confronting a victim (eg: mugging, purse snatching, extortion or armed robbery); or force someone into sexual activity. Physical violence may take the form of rape, assault, or in rare cases, homicide.'[10] The *DSM* explains that the symptoms of 'conduct disorder' vary with age. Less severe behaviours, such as lying, shoplifting, and fighting tend to emerge first, while the most severe conduct problems, such as rape and theft with violence, tend to emerge last.[11] In effect, the *DSM* is asserting that those who lie, steal, rape and murder are mentally ill, and therefore not entirely responsible for their actions.

The essential feature of 'oppositional defiant disorder' is a recurrent pattern of defiant, disobedient and hostile behaviour towards authority figures. Behaviour and attitudes that define this disorder are losing temper, arguing with adults, actively defying or refusing to comply with the requests or rules of adults, being touchy or easily annoyed by others, being angry, resentful, spiteful or vindictive.[12] The world of psychiatry, through the authority of the *DSM*, is asserting that the behaviour traits described above are symptoms of mental illness. The implication is that people with 'oppositional defiant disorder' are ill and therefore not really accountable for their behaviour.

But Scripture does not see the actions and attitudes that *DSM-IV* has chosen to label 'conduct disorder' and 'oppositional defiant disorder' as features of a mental illness. On the contrary, Scripture teaches that lying, stealing, violence, disobedience, rebellion, anger, rape and murder are sinful actions condemned by God's law – the fruit of an evil, rebellious heart. The Lord Jesus said, 'For from within, out of the heart of men, proceed evil thoughts, adulteries, fornications, murders, thefts, covetousness, wickedness, deceit, lewdness, an evil eye, blasphemy, pride, foolishness. All these evil things come from within and defile a man' *(Mark 7.21-23)*.

What we have described is a fundamental difference in the way the *DSM*, on the one hand, and Scripture, on the other hand, view the nature of man's problem. The *DSM*, from its stance in secular humanism, does not recognise the spiritual nature of man and has no understanding of the nature and consequences of sin. It seeks to persuade society that the people it labels with 'clinical depression', 'conduct disorder' or 'oppositional defiant disorder' are suffering with a disorder, and therefore are not altogether responsible for their actions and are in need of help from a psychiatrist or therapist.

The psycho-secular model of depression

We are now in a position to identify two essential characteristics of the model of depression constructed by the *DSM*. First, the model is *secular in approach,* in that it ignores the spiritual dimension of life. There is no recognition that man has a living soul, and is created in the image of God. There is no acknowledgement of man's sinful nature, or that sin has consequences.

Second, the model is *psychological in orientation* in that it is based on the wisdom of psychiatrists and counsellors steeped in the psychological theories that have come from the giants of psychotherapy, such as Freud, Adler, Maslow, Rogers and Ellis, among others. As a *secular, psychological model* it describes depression as a mental disease that affects our feelings, thoughts and actions. Depressed people need to be treated with drugs and psychotherapy.

The term *psycho-secular depression* accurately describes the characteristics of the *DSM* model created by the psychiatry profession. Its effect has been to move emotional despair from the spiritual realm into the secular world of psychiatry and psychotherapy.

Christians and depression

The Christian counselling movement has accepted without reservation the *psycho-secular* model of depression constructed by the *DSM*, and has propagated it widely throughout the Christian church in books, magazines, seminars, conferences and schools of theology.

An article in *Evangelicals Now* (March 1999) by Dr Klaus Green, entitled 'Notes on dealing with depressive illness', illustrates the commitment of many evangelicals to the *psycho-secular* model of depression. Dr Green explains that we all experience different moods and stresses at different times. 'We can find ourselves stressed by commitments, demands, tragedies and trials of various kinds. Perhaps it is as if a human being has an elastic band inside which feels the tension. These stresses cause a response in us. We feel "down" or "low" or "depressed" . . . In depressive illness it is as if our elastic band breaks, or at least get so stretched that it loses its power of recovery.'

Dr Green says that the church can help by accepting that *depression is an illness* and so it is not wrong for a Christian to be depressed. To help prevent depression the church must 'avoid letting willing individuals take on too much for the church. That one extra responsibility could be the last straw which pushes that person beyond their limit.' And Christians are assured that they should not worry about taking antidepressants. 'Yes, drugs like Prozac can be misused, but this should not rob us of their proper use. Antidepressants are not addictive. Depression often relates to a chemical imbalance in the brain and medication helps to restore the balance.'[13] Dr Green refers to medication as 'a God-given provision'.[14]

The significance of this article is that it encourages evangelical Christians to accept the *psycho-secular* model of depression. The simplistic argument is that as great men of God like Elijah, Jeremiah and Job suffered with mental illness, it is alright for Christians to suffer in the same way. What is depressing about the article is the way it handles Scripture. There is nothing in Scripture to suggest that the elastic bands of Elijah, Jeremiah and Job broke, or that they had a chemical imbalance in their brains. Nor did they receive any medication or therapy; they recovered without these. The advice that Christians should not 'take on too much for the church' directly contradicts biblical teaching. Did Christ not instruct his disciples to go the extra mile? Did Epaphroditus not risk his life for the Gospel *(Philippians 2.30)*? Did Paul not labour night and day for the Gospel of Christ, his beloved Saviour?

In a more recent article in *Evangelicals Now* (October 2008), Dr Mike Davies, a Christian GP, stresses that depression is a real medical condition. 'The first building block of our argument is to say that serious depression and anxiety disorders are real medical conditions that are faced by Christians and need to be viewed as such . . . While no one – to our knowledge – has separately studied the mental health of Christians in today's evangelical congregations, there is no reason to think that the incidence of mental health issues will be significantly less in our churches. Indeed, because our evangelical churches – quite rightly – provide environments that are caring and supportive, individuals with mental health issues may be attracted to them.'

Dr Davies recommends a 'range of helpful treatments that include both the use of antidepressant drugs or talking therapies . . .' He argues that the talking therapies such as Cognitive Behaviour Therapy (CBT, described in chapter 10) should not be dismissed because the models used are secular and not specifically Christian. 'In our experience as a GP practice, rightly used, the techniques derived from CBT can be very helpful in moderating the symptoms of what are often very debilitating conditions.'[15]

Christian psychiatrists, Dr Chris Williams and Dr Ingrid Whitton, with Baptist pastor Paul Richards, in *I'm Not Supposed to Feel Like This* (2002), underline the point that depression is an illness. 'When someone feels very low for more than two weeks and feels like this day after day, week after week, this is called depressive illness.'[16] They believe that the best approach to pastoral care for people with depression and other psychiatric conditions is to see it in the same way as any other physical illness. 'Depression and anxiety are not due to a lack of faith or a mistrust of God – they are illnesses and should be treated as such.'[17]

Dr Archibald D. Hart, Dean and Professor of Psychology of the Graduate School of Psychology, Fuller Theological Seminary, in his book *Dark Clouds, Silver Linings* (1993) seeks to help Christians understand depression and to overcome its devastating effects. 'If you're an average person, you will experience a significant depression some time in your life. Depression is epidemic in our society. Some call it the "common cold" of the emotions. At some time in their lives, one in every five people will experience depression seriously enough to hinder their normal way of life. It can increase feelings of insecurity, low self-esteem, and helplessness. But depression doesn't have to rule your life.'[18]

According to Hart, when we finally realise that we are in depression's grasp, 'it has already sapped our strength to fight it and fogged our minds to understand it. It knocks us flat before we have a chance to put up a defence. Strangely enough, he observes, only about one-third of those seriously depressed will actually seek treatment. Some don't know they can be helped. Some don't accurately label what they're feeling. Most don't seek treatment because they're too depressed and feel too helpless and hopeless to believe they can get better. Many choose to "tough it out" for months or even years rather than get treatment. Among these untreated depressed persons are, of course, many Christians. They don't realise that with the right sort of treatment, they could probably bounce back in a matter of weeks, and many could prevent any reoccurring episodes of depression. Their failure to get help is sad.'[19] Hart's plea is for depressed Christians to seek medical treatment for their depression just like everybody else.

Christian psychiatrists Frank Minirth and Paul Meier discuss the symptoms, causes and cures of depression in their bestseller *Happiness is a Choice* (1994). Who gets depressed? 'At some period of life, nearly

everyone does! Our strong contention, however, is tha
suffering from a serious clinical depression can find
is a way out of the pain. Depression (without bic
usually curable with the right kind of therapeutic help.'[20] They ...
depression as a devastating illness that affects the total being – physical, emotional and spiritual. The good news, according to Minirth and
Meier, is that 'anyone can be cured of a clinical depression if he becomes
actively involved in good-quality professional psychotherapy'. There is
no doubt that Minirth and Meier speak for the Christian counselling
movement: all Christians are in danger of suffering with depression,
but can be cured provided they receive the right kind of therapy.

Minirth and Meier offer a self-rating scale of depression with the
advice that anyone who answers 'true' to a majority of the questions
is almost certainly depressed and should seek professional assistance
before the depression worsens. The 18 symptoms that make up the
rating scale include, I feel blue and sad; I am losing my appetite; I am
too irritable; I worry about the past; I have less energy than usual; my
sleep pattern has changed of late – I either sleep too much or too little;
my self-concept is not very good; and so on.[21] We can only wonder how
many people will use this scale and become convinced that they need
professional help to overcome what they are encouraged to conclude is
their depression.

In his book *Christian Counselling*, Gary Collins, a prominent
American Christian psychologist, draws attention to the problem of the
person who has many of the symptoms of depression but denies that he
or she feels sad. 'In what is sometimes known as masked depression, the
alert counsellor may suspect that depression is present even behind a
smiling countenance.'[22] So the task of the alert counsellor is to uncover
masked depression even among those who deny feeling sad. Here it is
not difficult to see that the alert counsellor, on the look-out for masked
depression, will be able to find signs and symptoms of depression in
virtually all who come for counselling.

James Dobson believes that low self-esteem is a major cause of
depression in women. He also advises that 'antidepressant drugs are
highly effective in controlling most cases of severe depression. He
acknowledges that medication will not correct the circumstances
which precipitated her original problems, and the possibility of low

lf-esteem and other causes must be faced and dealt with, perhaps with the help of a psychologist or psychiatrist.'[23]

David Seamands claims that often 'the roots of depression are buried in the subsoil of early family life. And unless you learn to deal honestly with those angry roots, to face your resentment and forgive, you'll be living in a greenhouse where depression is sure to flourish.'[24] We must face up to the fact that there may be frozen anger somewhere in our lives. 'Towards parents? Family members? Are you angry at God? So many people need to forgive God, not because he has ever done anything wrong, but because they have held him responsible.'[25]

The above discussion shows that the Christian counselling movement has accepted the *psycho-secular* view of depression at face value. What is noticeable is the vast range of circumstances that can cause this 'disease', from low self-esteem to a chemical imbalance; from not sleeping well to inappropriate guilt or dwelling on past wrongs. The problem with this approach is that virtually the whole population will be caught in the depression net. Even those who don't feel depressed may be told by a therapist that they have masked depression. It seems highly probable that the psycho-secular approach will lead to many Christians being labelled and treated for depression. Perhaps now we can understand why there is an epidemic of depression even among Christians.

A consultant in psychological medicine, Alastair M. Santhouse, makes the point: 'A growing number of patients I see who have gained a diagnosis of depression, or who have failed to respond to treatment, are not really depressed at all. More detailed questioning reveals a familiar pattern in which the patient lacks a sense of purpose in life, with no higher goals or aspirations. Naturally this is accompanied by symptoms associated with depression, such as sadness, pessimism, or hopelessness – but identifying these symptoms simply as a biological depression misses the point entirely. Antidepressants do not help to give the patient a sense of purpose. We must speak to the person behind the symptoms and discover what will give their lives meaning.'[26]

The chemical imbalance hypothesis

The idea of a chemical imbalance is accepted as an important underlying cause of *psycho-secular* depression. According to this theory, a chemical imbalance of the neurotransmitters in the brain causes depression, just as a low level of insulin causes diabetes. The chemical imbalance theory, not surprisingly, is widely quoted by drug companies that produce antidepressant drugs. For example, a website sponsored by GlaxoSmithKline asserts that 'depression is not something you can just "snap out of". It's caused by an imbalance of brain chemicals, along with other factors. Like any serious medical condition, depression needs to be treated.' Depression can make you feel hopeless and help-less. But just taking the first step – deciding to get treatment – can make all the difference. In the USA the television advertising campaign for Zoloft, one of the most popular new antidepressant medications, says that 'although its cause is unknown, depression may be caused by an imbalance in the chemistry of the brain'.[27]

Yet there is no diagnostic test for determining whether or not someone has a chemical imbalance. While norepinephrine and sero-tonin are the two neurotransmitters most commonly associated with mood disorders, there is currently no way to measure the levels of these two chemicals in the brain. Instead, doctors look for metabolites, which are the by-products left behind after the neurotransmitters are broken down.[28] But this is hardly a valid and reliable measure of the levels of the chemicals involved in neurotransmission. Moreover, as the levels of these chemicals are changing all the time, we don't even know their normal physiological range, let alone what is pathologically high or low.

Notwithstanding, the idea of a chemical imbalance has been so widely promoted that it has entered popular consciousness. Drug companies which produce antidepressants have made much of the imbalance theory. In the USA millions of viewers have seen a TV advertisement in which a bouncing ball turns from a sad face to a happy face as the voice-over claims that an antidepressant helps correct a chemical imbalance. The message is simple: drugs restore the brain's chemical balance.

The American Association of Christian Counsellors, which claims that more than 16 per cent of the population suffers from depres-sion severe enough to warrant treatment at some time in their lives, goes along with the chemical imbalance hypothesis. According to the Association (we saw these words elsewhere), 'Depression is not some-thing you can just snap out of. It's caused by an imbalance of brain chemicals, along with other factors. Like any serious medical condi-tion, depression needs to be treated.' Therefore, 'it is OK for you to take medications if needed to get depression under control. It doesn't mean you are weak or don't have enough faith. It is possible that the depression is biochemical and that medication can straighten out the chemicals in your body and help you get over the depression.'[29]

The notion of the chemical imbalance is commonly believed and promoted among Christians. Dr Ann Shorb, an experienced Christian counsellor, runs a private counselling group called Christian Counselling and Educational Services. In workshops called 'Dealing with Depression', after explaining that the Bible is full of stories of people who suffered from depression, she teaches that internal depression is triggered by a chemical imbalance in the brain. The Bible won't help people who have a chemical imbalance until the underlying physical problem is treated. In those cases, she refers her clients to a psychiatrist who can prescribe medications. She tells her audience that medication gives people a jump start.[30]

Many Christian seminars on *psycho-secular* depression in the UK promote this line of thinking. The usual claim is that the chemical imbalance theory is supported by sound scientific research. As a consequence most Christians are persuaded that the chemical imbalance is a proven scientific fact. It follows that Christians are just as prone to a chemical imbalance as anyone else and therefore need the benefits that come from antidepressant drugs.

However, both the drug companies and the Christian counselling movement are presenting a grossly misleading picture, for the chemical imbalance hypothesis is not supported by the scientific evidence. In their paper 'Serotonin and Depression: A Disconnect between the Advertisements and the Scientific Literature', two eminent researchers – Jeffrey Lacasse, of Florida State University and Dr Jonathan Leo, a neuroanatomy professor at Lake Erie College of Osteopathic Medicine* – debunk the chemical imbalance hypothesis. According to the authors, 'to propose that researchers can objectively identify a "chemical imbalance" at the molecular level is not compatible with the extant science. In fact, there is no scientifically established ideal "chemical balance" of serotonin, let alone an identifiable pathological

---

* These two scientists have examined the link between consumer advertisements for selective serotonin reuptake inhibitor (SSRI) antidepressants that claimed these drugs restore the serotonin balance of the brain, and the published scientific evidence.

imbalance.' The authors summed up their paper with these words: 'In short, there exists no rigorous corroboration of the serotonin theory . . . doubts about the serotonin hypothesis are well acknowledged by many researchers . . . there is not a single peer-reviewed article that can be accurately cited to directly support claims of serotonin deficiency in any mental disorder, while there are many articles that present counterevidence.'[31]

In view of the lack of scientific evidence to support the chemical imbalance hypothesis, the Irish Medicines Board has recently banned GlaxoSmithKline from claiming in their patient information leaflets that paroxetine (Paxil) corrects a chemical imbalance. (The American FDA has never taken any similar action on this issue.) Commenting on Lacasse and Leo's work, Professor David Healy of the North Wales Department of Psychological Medicine said: 'The serotonin theory of depression is comparable to the masturbatory theory of insanity. Both have been depletion theories, both have survived in spite of the evidence, both contain an implicit message as to what people ought to do. In the case of these myths, the key question is whose interests are being served by a widespread promulgation of such views rather than how do we test this theory.'[32]

Dr Joanna Moncrieff, Senior Lecturer in Psychiatry at University College London, said: 'It is high time that it was stated clearly that the serotonin imbalance theory of depression is not supported by the scientific evidence or by expert opinion. Through misleading publicity the pharmaceutical industry has helped to ensure that most of the general public is unaware of this.'[33] Her book *The Myth of the Chemical Cure* (2007) exposes the traditional view that psychiatric drugs correct chemical imbalances as a dangerous fraud. She argues that the chemical imbalance theory supports the vested interests of the psychiatric profession, the pharmaceutical industry and the modern state. Dr Moncrieff argues that 'the marketing of antidepressants has persuaded a large proportion of the population of Western countries to take prescribed drugs to deal with the problems of living . . . The message that drugs can cure your problems has profound consequences. It encourages people to view themselves as powerless victims of their biology, and stores up untold misery for the future when people come to realise that their problems have not gone away but [they] have failed to develop more constructive ways of dealing with them.'[34]

And here we must ask the question, Why have Christian counsellors been so keen to accept and promote the chemical imbalance hypothesis? By doing so they are joining with the drug companies in encouraging millions of people to turn to psychotropic drugs in an attempt to find an answer for their unhappiness. Moncrieff makes the point that drug treatment in people seeking help for 'depression' is of little value. 'The reduced emotional sensitivity associated with the use of any psycho-active substance may bring temporary relief to someone who is very distressed, but it is unlikely to help them to uncover and deal with the source of their problems. What people who are depressed or unhappy really need is help and support from other human beings.'[35]

Conclusion

The *psycho-secular* model of depression has broadened the diagnostic criteria so wide that a large section of the population is at risk of being labelled clinically depressed. A direct consequence has been a massive increase in the number of Christians diagnosed with depression. The response of the church has been to create a Christian counselling movement to help depressed Christians deal with their troubled spirits.

Many therapists, both secular and Christian, now believe that cognitive therapy is the most effective treatment for depression. Consequently, large numbers of Christians are referred to a Christian counsellor to receive psychotherapy. Yet there is a question that needs to be asked. Is it possible that depression is being over diagnosed and that unhappy Christians are receiving unnecessary treatments?

Why are Christians so eager to accept the *psycho-secular* model of depression that has emerged from the mindset of secular humanism? The fact that evangelical Christians, who are supposed to live by the Scriptures, are prepared to embrace the widespread use of antidepressants and cognitive therapy to help depressed Christians shows how confused our thinking has become. The reason we have gone so wrong is because our thinking has not been rooted and grounded in Scripture. We have followed too closely the ideas of men; we have been influenced by the spirit of the age. In the next chapter we examine a biblical response to the issue of *psycho-secular depression*.

3
The Biblical View of Depression

IN THE PREVIOUS CHAPTER we saw that the *psycho-secular disease* model of depression, developed by the *DSM* of the American Psychiatric Association, is now widely accepted by many Christians. There is no doubt that the Christian counselling movement has succeeded in inculcating the *psycho-secular* view of depression right into the heart of the Christian church. This is why books on how to overcome depression are bestsellers, and why depression seminars and counsellors are part of the ministry of many churches.

Christians who accept the view of depression developed by the world of psychiatry often turn to Scripture to justify their position, as we saw in the previous chapter. We are told that as great men of God showed signs of depression (Elijah, Job, Moses, Jonah and Jeremiah being quoted as examples), it is only to be expected that ordinary Christians will suffer in the same way. The inference is that the *psycho-secular* view of depression is supported by Scripture.

As a consequence there is now confusion around the issue of depression in the churches. Why are there so many supposedly depressed people needing counselling or other treatment in church congregations? Are they all really suffering with a mental illness? Or should we distinguish more clearly between truly serious depression and simply feeling low? Many sense that it cannot be right for so many Christians to be receiving psychotherapy from secular therapists to help them deal with problems of daily living, and some question whether Christians need antidepressant drugs to help them overcome their depressed feelings. After all, Scripture promises that God's divine power has given us all things that pertain to life and godliness through the knowledge of Christ *(2 Peter 1.3)*. Adding to the confusion is the fact that the word 'depression' is used nowadays to describe a wide range of emotional responses.

To understand the issue of depression and to overcome our confusion we must start with Scripture, and not with the ideas that come from the *DSM*. Scripture is profitable for instruction in righteous living 'that the man of God may be complete, thoroughly equipped for every good work' *(2 Timothy 3.16-17)*. A theme that runs through the Bible is that God's servants are often downcast and in deep despair. When Jacob was told that his son Joseph had been devoured by a wild beast he refused to be comforted and said, 'I shall go down into the grave to my son in mourning' *(Genesis 37.35)*. Scripture shows that Jacob was deeply depressed by the loss of his son. Clearly the Bible has a lot to say on the subject. So let us clear our minds of the presuppositions that come from the flawed *psycho-secular* approach to depression and turn to God's Word with an eager, expectant mind. Let us search the Scriptures to understand what the Bible has to say about 'depression'.

The depression of King David

In the *Psalms*, King David gives full vent to his episodes of depression. In *Psalm 13* David describes the daily sorrow in his heart because he feels forgotten by God. 'How long, O Lord? Will You forget me forever? How long will You hide Your face from me? How long shall I take counsel in my soul, having sorrow in my heart daily?' *(Psalm 13.1-2)*. The pain in David's heart comes from a sense that God has forgotten him. He feels that he is walking in darkness, distant from God, and this is the cause of his ongoing despair. Matthew Henry explains, 'God sometimes hides his face, and leaves his own children in the dark concerning their interest in him: and this they lay to heart more than any outward trouble whatever.' David's response to his downcast feelings is to trust in God's mercy, and to rejoice in God's salvation (v5).

In *Psalm 31* King David expresses his profound grief as a result of the slander of his enemies and schemes against his life and because of his own sin. 'Have mercy on me, O Lord, for I am in trouble; my eye wastes away with grief, yes, my soul and my body! For my life is spent with grief, and my years with sighing; my strength fails because of my iniquity, and my bones waste away . . . I am forgotten like a dead man, out of mind; I am like a broken vessel' *(Psalm 31.9-10, 12)*. David is a man in distress and trouble. And his great concern is about his soul. His response is to affirm his trust in God. And he gives this encouragement to those who are downcast, 'Be of good courage, and He shall strengthen your heart, all you who hope in the Lord' *(Psalm 31.24)*.

David describes his deep despair when betrayed by his friend and counsellor Ahithophel. 'My heart is severely pained within me, and the terrors of death have fallen upon me. Fearfulness and trembling have come upon me, and horror has overwhelmed me' *(Psalm 55.4-5)*. In his deep despondency David longs for wings like a dove to fly from his torment – the realisation that it is his friend who has betrayed him. Then he comes to his senses and calls upon God. 'And the Lord shall save me. Evening and morning and at noon I will pray, and cry aloud, and He shall hear my voice . . . Cast your burden on the Lord, and He shall sustain you; He shall never permit the righteous to be moved' *(Psalm 55.16-17, 22)*.

Psalm 38 is a prayer for deliverance from God's chastening for his sins. 'I am troubled, I am bowed down greatly; I go mourning all the day long. For my loins are full of inflammation, and there is no soundness in my flesh. I am feeble and severely broken; I groan because of the turmoil of my heart . . . For I am ready to fall, and my sorrow is continually before me. For I will declare my iniquity; I will be in anguish over my sin' *(Psalm 38.6-8, 17-18)*. Scripture is up-front that David's turmoil of heart, his continuous sorrow and anguish, is here caused by his iniquity and sin.

King David despised the commandment of the Lord when he committed adultery with Bathsheba and murdered Uriah her husband. His sin had the most severe spiritual consequences – he lost the joy of salvation, he no longer knew God's presence, his sin was always before him, he had a guilty conscience and a broken heart. David describes his despair in *Psalm 51* as he confesses his terrible sin to God – 'against You, You only, have I sinned' – and prays that God would wash him clean and deliver him from the guilt of bloodshed. 'Make me hear joy and gladness, that the bones You have broken may rejoice . . . Restore to me the joy of Your salvation' *(Psalm 51.8, 12)*. Here we have a clear example of the consequences of sin in the life of a believer. We also have the answer to despair caused by sin – confession and repentance.

Those who accept the *psycho-secular* approach would say that David's symptoms were consistent with a diagnosis of clinical depression. But Scripture shows that David's downcast feelings were a spiritual condition – he was not suffering from a mental illness or a chemical disorder of the brain. In *Psalm 13* the daily sorrow in his heart was caused by the feeling that God had forgotten him; he felt that he was walking in darkness. In *Psalm 55* his severely pained heart, his fearfulness and trembling, was caused by difficult, adverse circumstances. In *Psalms 38* and *51* David makes it clear that he was greatly cast down because of his sin – 'my sorrow is continually before me. For I will declare my iniquity; I will be in anguish over my sin.' In *Psalm 31* David wasted away with grief because of both adverse circumstances and sin. Clearly, the biblical picture of 'depression' is very different from that described by the *DSM*. We are, in fact, dealing with two different, and fundamentally opposed, views of human emotions.

The *psycho-secular* view of depression is based on the *DSM*, a manual rooted in secular humanism, but regarded by many as the 'bible' of psychiatry. *Psycho-secular* depression denies the spiritual dimension of man and rejects the doctrine of original sin. According to this view, man is an evolved animal without a spiritual dimension to his life. Depression is often due to a mysterious chemical imbalance that produces a disorder of the brain that results in mental illness. The *biblical* view of depression flows out of the fact that man is a living soul created in the image of God and accountable for his actions. All are sinners by nature and sin has consequences that affect our behaviour, thoughts and emotions. King David experienced sorrow and despair because of adverse circumstances and sin. God also allowed him to walk in darkness to test and strengthen his faith.

While Scripture has much to say on the subject of 'depression' it does not use the term. Instead it uses various phrases, such as a downcast soul, deeply distressed, walking in darkness, a sorrowful spirit, a grieving heart, bitterness of soul, all these terms describing the suffering of a depressed soul. Moreover, Scripture and the *DSM* have different views of the causes of depression, as we have already seen, and the response of men of God such as David, Job and Jeremiah, is fundamentally different from the response advocated by the *DSM*. So the only similarity between a *psycho-secular* view of depression and the *biblical* view of depression is that both involve the same type of symptoms. We are, in fact, dealing with two fundamentally opposed views of depression, founded in fundamentally opposed worldviews. The battle over the interpretation of depression is, ultimately, a spiritual battle between the forces of secular humanism and the truth of God's Word.

In order to distinguish between two fundamentally opposed views of depression, we need to use terminology that makes the distinction clear. To use the same term, 'depression', to describe two entirely different and opposing concepts is a recipe for muddled thinking. There is no doubt that the all-embracing term 'depression' has led to a great deal of confusion, for it is being interpreted in different ways and means different things to different people. Moreover, there is always the spectre of mental illness lurking around the term 'depression'. Here it is important to point out that while a small proportion of patients with serious symptoms of depression have a genuine mental illness and may benefit from medical treatment, the vast majority are not mentally ill.

To distinguish between the two opposing views we use the term *psycho-secular depression* to describe the model constructed by the *DSM*, and terms used in the Bible, namely, *downcast soul, deep despair* or *walking in darkness*, to describe the biblical view. (The Puritans used the term *melancholia*.)

The emotional nature of man

Scripture teaches that the eternal God, revealed in the incarnate Christ, has an emotional aspect to his character. The Lord Jesus exhibited the full range of human emotions, although without sin. He was joyful, he wept over Jerusalem, he was greatly troubled by the death of Lazarus, he loved the rich young man, and he was angry and grieved at the hardness of heart of the Pharisees. In the Garden of Gethsemane he was troubled; his soul was exceedingly sorrowful and deeply distressed

(Mark 14.33, 34). Scripture teaches that man, created in the image of God, is a living soul with the ability to experience and express a range of emotions. In *The Origin of Man*, Stuart Burgess explains that our uniquely created facial muscles allow us to express emotions such as happiness, disapproval, confusion, grief, anger, pain, surprise and boredom. The ability to cry is a uniquely human attribute from a Creator who has created man in such a way that he is able to express his emotional feelings.[1]

The effect of the Fall on human emotions

In their state of innocence in the Garden of Eden, Adam and Eve were perfectly content for they knew the joy of communion with God. When Adam and Eve sinned they became separated from the presence of God. Their emotional life was seriously impaired, for they felt afraid, ashamed and guilty. Their relationship became troubled as Adam blamed his wife for their condition. Life outside Eden, banished from God's presence, was difficult, frustrating, painful and sorrowful. Men would tend to rule over women. Brothers would be filled with envy, anger and hatred – such as downcast Cain who killed his brother Abel. The Fall had a catastrophic effect on the human condition. From henceforth all people would experience physical and emotional suffering. All men, because of their sinful nature, are subject to trouble, despair, despondency and sadness. Men and women needed to be saved from their slavery to sin.

Adam and Eve, had they filled in a screening questionnaire, would undoubtedly have been diagnosed as suffering with clinical depression by today's mental health industry, for they had deep feelings of sadness and a very marked loss of pleasure as they hid from the presence of God among the trees of the Garden, filled with fear, guilt and shame. A psychotherapist would have confirmed the diagnosis and prescribed a course of cognitive therapy. But Scripture makes it clear that their wretched condition, their *downcast soul*, was caused by their separation from God. They needed a Saviour, not a therapist.

To understand the deep-seated nature of mankind's problem we must see it in the context of the Fall. In his volume of systematic theology Robert Reymond explains, 'Every part of his being – his mind, his will, his *emotions*, his affections, his conscience, his body – has been affected by sin (this is what is meant by the doctrine of total depravity). His understanding is darkened, his mind is at enmity with God, his will to act is slave to this darkened understanding and rebellious mind, his heart is corrupt, *his emotions are perverted* [my italics], his affections naturally gravitate to that which is evil and ungodly, his conscience is untrustworthy and his body is subject to mortality.'[2] He is spiritually dead and his body is subject to disease and decay.

The Fall has also affected the world in which man lives. The creation is subject to futility and the bondage of corruption. 'For we know that the whole creation groans and labours with birth pangs together until now' *(Romans 8.22)*. The ground is cursed and brings forth thorns and thistles. The life of man is governed by sweat and toil. Even Christians, who have the indwelling Spirit, groan within themselves as they wait for the redemption of their bodies *(Romans 8.23)*. We experience the sorrow of living each day with the burden of the world, our flesh, and our mind that so easily leads us into sins we have no desire to commit. 'But what I hate, that I do ... O wretched man that I am! Who will deliver me from this body of death?' *(Romans 7.15, 24)*. Our bodies are part of creation and participate in all the futility and corruption to which creation has been subjected. In this life, this side of Heaven, there are days of trouble and difficulty. 'Man who is born of woman is of few days and full of trouble' *(Job 14.1)*. Moreover, the Lord Jesus warned that the life of a disciple is subject to persecution. He said plainly that 'in the world you will have tribulation' *(John 16.33)*.

As a consequence of the Fall the human mind is troubled and unable to find rest and contentment. There are many hardships, for life in a fallen world, governed by sin and corruption, is full of frustration and strife. The spirit of man is subject to continuing unease with the way things are; persistent feelings that the world is not quite right, that it is a place of suffering, foolishness, and evil. Despair and sadness may sometimes be the lot of a Christian who grows weary of the constant spiritual battle 'against the rulers of the darkness of this age, against spiritual hosts of wickedness in the heavenly places' *(Ephesians 6.12)*.

Diseases of the brain and mental illness

Another consequence of the Fall is that man's body is subject to disease and decay. We see this in organic diseases of the brain such as epilepsy, Parkinson's disease, brain tumours and dementia. But what about mental disorders created by the *DSM*, such as depression and conduct disorder, which have no organic pathology? As we saw in chapter 2, there is no objective test to confirm the diagnosis of clinical depression. Because the subjective data gathered from the patient is inherently unreliable, it is difficult for the clinician to be certain that the symptoms are caused by a mental disease. A report of the USA Surgeon General acknowledges the difficulty in diagnosing depression. He makes the point that for 'mental disorders such as depression, the signs and symptoms exist on a continuum and there is no bright line separating health from illness, distress from disease'.[3]

Scripture confirms the difficulty in diagnosing mental illness. When David fled before Saul he ended up in Gath. He was very much afraid of King Achish, 'so he changed his behaviour before them, pretended madness in their hands, scratched on the doors of the gate, and let his saliva fall down on his beard' *(1 Samuel 21.13)*. David's pretence of insanity was so convincing that the king and his servants were completely deceived. King Achish said to his servants, 'Have I need of madmen, that you have brought this fellow to play the madman in my presence?' (v15). Clearly it is possible for a person to feign mental illness for his own purposes.

While recognising the diagnostic difficulties, it is important to again state that a small group of people with the most severe symptoms of depression are likely to benefit from medical treatment. Some people may also experience alarming symptoms such as hallucinations and delusions, even endangering their own lives or those of others, and these require medical attention. Hallucinations occur when an individual experiences a sensory impression that has no basis in reality. A delusion is a false belief that an individual holds despite evidence to the contrary. A common example is paranoia, in which a person has delusional beliefs that others are trying to harm him. Attempts to persuade the person that these beliefs are unfounded typically fail and may even result in the further entrenchment of the delusional beliefs.[4]

According to the report of the Surgeon General, patients with psychotic disorders such as schizophrenia frequently have marked disturbances in the logical process of their thoughts. 'Specifically, psychotic thought processes are characteristically loose, disorganised, illogical, or bizarre. These disturbances in thought process frequently produce observable patterns of behaviour that are also disorganised and bizarre. The severe disturbances of thought content and process that comprise the positive symptoms often are the most recognisable and striking features of psychotic disorders such as schizophrenia or manic depressive illness.'[5]

Undoubtedly the small proportion of depressed people who exhibit the symptoms mentioned above have a genuine need for medical treatment. But we need to keep the issue in perspective, for the vast majority of people who are given a label of clinical depression by the counselling industry are not in need of medical treatment. We can be confident that the claim of the counselling world that ten per cent of the population, each year, suffer with clinical depression is false – there is no doubt that the condition is being massively over diagnosed.

Examples from Scripture of a downcast soul

There are many examples in Scripture of men and women who experienced deep despair, misery, sadness, despondency and a downcast soul, symptoms that would today be wrongly diagnosed as depressive illness – what we are calling psycho-secular depression. From Scripture we can identify three broad groups of people who suffered from these symptoms. The first are those downcast because of adverse circumstances, such as those experienced by Job and Hannah. The second are those who walk in darkness or gloom as a result of living in a fallen world. The third are in deep despair because of their personal sin, such as King Saul and Cain. However, these are broad categories with considerable overlap, for all people are subject to the consequences of living in a fallen world. Adverse circumstances and sin often go together. Nevertheless, to think about the causes of spiritual and emotional suffering in these groups will help our understanding.

Here we should remind ourselves yet again of the difference between psycho-secular depression and the biblical view of a downcast soul. Psycho-secular depression is the brainchild of psychiatry. It denies the spiritual nature of man; it denies the reality and consequences of the Fall; it treats depression with psychotherapy and drugs. The biblical concept of a downcast soul, by contrast, accepts the spiritual nature of man. It recognises the effect of the spiritual Fall, and the oppressive consequences of sin. The answer to a downcast soul is always found in the Word of God. While the two views have a common understanding of the symptoms of 'depression', they differ radically in their understanding of the causes and the response to these symptoms.

(1) A soul downcast by adverse circumstances
(a) The apostle Paul burdened beyond measure

In his *Second Letter to the Corinthians* Paul describes his suffering in the cause of Christ, there being 30 references to the despair that the great apostle endured in the name of Christ. The apostle wants the Corinthian church to know of the great hardship he suffered during his missionary journey in Asia. Such were the sufferings and troubles of Paul and his companions that they 'were burdened beyond measure, above strength, so that we despaired even of life' *(2 Corinthians 1.8)*. But God allowed this to happen, according to Paul, 'that we should not trust in ourselves but in God who raises the dead' *(2 Corinthians 1.9)*. The message is that during times of profound suffering and difficulty we should trust in God.

Paul refers to his 'anguish of heart' and 'many tears' *(2 Corinthians 2.4)* in dealing with the Corinthian church. When they arrived in Macedonia they were downcast because 'our bodies had no rest, but we were troubled on every side. Outside were conflicts, inside were fears. Nevertheless God, who comforts the downcast, comforted us by the coming of Titus' *(2 Corinthians 7.5-6)*. Paul gives a detailed list of what he suffered for the sake of Christ. He was often whipped and beaten with rods; he was stoned and shipwrecked; he was frequently in perils from robbers, from false brethren, from Gentiles and even his own countrymen. He suffered weariness and toil, sleeplessness, hunger and thirst, cold and nakedness, besides the other troubles that came upon him daily *(2 Corinthians 11.24-28)*. Paul is making it clear that hardship and suffering, both emotional and physical, *are a part of the Christian life.*

God had allowed Paul to have a thorn in his flesh. And when Paul asked God to remove the thorn, God said, 'My grace is sufficient for you, for My strength is made perfect in weakness' *(2 Corinthians 12.9)*. With this promise from God, Paul could take pleasure in infirmities, in reproaches, in needs, in persecutions, in distresses, for Christ's sake.

Paul's response was to place his trust in the God of all comfort, for he had learned to be content whatever his circumstances. He knew that God's grace was sufficient.

In his book, *Pain of Mind: A Biblical Perspective of Depression,* Dr Earl Cooper concludes that in the second letter to the Corinthian church Paul wraps up emotional despondency, extreme burdens, and intolerable affliction in one bundle and designates it suffering. 'It is to this end that the epistle offers such practical insight to the suffering believer, whether suffering from physical illness or the stress of circumstances or from the emotional upheaval, Paul's view of suffering lays down a biblical foundation for victory.'[6] Cooper explains that Paul relates his personal struggle, including emotional despondency, in terms of the importance of prayer, dependence upon God, and the sufficiency of God. 'His proper handling of life's difficulties was not release from suffering, but strength from God in suffering. Paul's acceptance of suffering and weakness, indeed, his welcoming of such for the sake of the glory of God, flies in the face of today's fretful saints. All believers, whether undergoing stressful circumstances, physical affliction, or emotional despondency, would benefit from a closer look at the theology of suffering.'[7]

Paul not only accepted suffering as a part of serving Christ, he viewed it as a privilege to suffer for his Lord. He wanted to know Christ, and to share in the fellowship of his sufferings *(Philippians 3.10)*. It is interesting that the Christian counselling movement never uses Paul as an example of a depressed Christian, although in his letters he frequently mentioned the despair and anguish that he suffered for the sake of the Gospel. Paul's witness is a model of how a true believer responds to a soul downcast by adverse circumstances.

(b) Hannah's sorrow of spirit

Childless Hannah was severely provoked by her rival Peninnah, who had many children by Elkanah, their husband. Scripture describes Hannah's mental turmoil in careful detail in the first chapter of *1 Samuel.* 'And her rival also provoked her severely, to make her miserable, because the Lord had closed her womb' *(1 Samuel 1.6)*. In her despair Hannah wept and did not eat (v7), and such was her sadness that her husband asked why her heart was grieved (v8). In bitterness of soul she prayed to the Lord and wept in anguish (v10). When she was confronted by Eli, and accused of being drunk, she answered, 'No, my lord, I am a woman of sorrowful spirit' (v15). When Eli assured her that the God of Israel would grant her petition, she went her way and ate and her face was no longer sad (vv17, 18).

Notice how Scripture emphasises Hannah's emotional suffering. She was miserable and had no appetite, her heart was grieved, she wept in anguish, and she had bitterness of soul and a sorrowful spirit. A Christian counsellor who follows the secular view of depression would diagnose a serious case of mental illness that required treatment, perhaps a course of antidepressants and cognitive therapy. However, Scripture shows that her profound despair was a spiritual matter, for God was teaching her to trust him; here we have a classic case of a *downcast* soul. Hannah's response was to trust in God, and the Lord remembered her and she bore a son. She called him Samuel, because she had asked for him from the Lord *(1 Samuel 1.20)*.

(c) The groaning of Job

God's servant Job went through extreme suffering because of the tragic events that God allowed Satan to inflict on him. Such was his suffering that Job cursed the day he was born. He experienced fear, misery and dread; he sighed and groaned in his despair *(Job 3)*. In his distress and after the taunt of his wife to curse God and die, Job understood that his adversity was from God. At the height of adverse circumstances and his terrible suffering, he fell to the ground and worshipped God: 'The Lord gave, and the Lord has taken away; blessed be the name of the Lord' *(Job 1.21)*.

Job experienced darkness of the soul and felt deserted by God. 'Look, I go forward, but He is not there, and backward, but I cannot perceive Him; when He works on the left hand, I cannot behold Him; when He turns to the right hand, I cannot see Him. But He knows the way that I take; when He has tested me, I shall come forth as gold . . . I have not departed from the commandment of His lips; I have treasured the words of His mouth more than my necessary food' *(Job 23.8-10, 12)*.

Despite his doubts in trying to understand why God had allowed him to suffer so much, Job retained his faith in God. After God spoke to Job – 'Would you condemn Me that you may be justified?' – Job repented of his poor attitude, 'Therefore I abhor myself, and repent in dust and ashes' *(Job 40.8* and *42.6)*. To equate Job's response to his torment with clinical depression, as the Christian counselling movement does, is to misinterpret Scripture – rather we see in Job an example of deep despair caused by adverse circumstances ordained by God himself. A Christian has much to learn from the example of Job, a man whose core faith in God did not waver even in the face of the most terrible suffering and trials. Job's testimony is given for our comfort.

(d) Jeremiah, the suffering prophet

The prophet Jeremiah experienced adverse circumstances when he was scorned and mocked. His life was threatened, he was put in the stocks and later he was thrown into a dark muddy pit. In his struggle he cursed the day he was born. 'Why did I come forth from the womb to see labour and sorrow, that my days should be consumed with shame?' *(Jeremiah 20.18)*. Yet the great prophet found victory over his despair, for he trusted the promise of God – 'For I am with you to save you and deliver you' *(Jeremiah 15.20)*. Jeremiah was able to gain victory over his suffering, caused by adverse circumstances, through his faith in God's promises. When he faced the greatest trial, when his adversaries were waiting for him to slip so that they could prevail over him, when all was against him, Jeremiah had this testimony, 'The Lord is with me as a mighty, awesome One' *(Jeremiah 20.11)*. He placed his faith in his Lord who had said, 'Blessed is the man who trusts in the Lord, and whose hope is the Lord. For he shall be like a tree planted by the waters, which spreads out its roots by the river, and will not fear when heat comes; but its leaf will be green, and will not be anxious in the year of drought, nor will cease from yielding fruit' *(Jeremiah 17.7-8)*. Jeremiah's faith in God, in the face of adverse circumstances, made him like a tree planted by the waters that was able to overcome both the heat and the drought of suffering.

The biblical response to despair that comes from adverse circumstances is to cleave to God and trust his promises. We must not despise the chastening of the Lord, for whom the Lord loves he disciplines and he does so for our profit that we may be partakers of his holiness *(Hebrews 12)*. While we cannot always understand why God allows his people to suffer adverse circumstances, we must, like Paul, Job,

Jeremiah and David, trust the God who has promised that in the face of our enemies he will not leave us alone. 'He will be with you, He will not leave you nor forsake you; do not fear nor be dismayed' *(Deuteronomy 31.8)*. Even though we walk through the valley of the shadow of death, God is with us. Our God 'heals the brokenhearted and binds up their wounds' *(Psalm 147.3)*.

(2) A soul walking in darkness

Scripture describes a condition of misery in a true believer for which there is no obvious cause. The prophet Isaiah describes the man of God who is obedient to God's commands yet is walking in darkness. 'Who among you fears the Lord? Who obeys the voice of His Servant? Who walks in darkness and has no light? Let him trust in the name of the Lord and rely upon his God' *(Isaiah 50.10)*. The word translated *darkness* comes from the Hebrew word *haseka*, which figuratively means *misery*. The prophet is speaking of the person who fears the Lord, and obeys his voice, yet is experiencing profound misery in his walk with God. Matthew Henry comments on the text: 'A sincere servant of God may for a long time be without views of eternal happiness. What is likely to be an effectual cure in this sad case? Let him trust in the name of the Lord; and let him stay himself upon the promises of the covenant, and build his hopes on them . . . A godly man's way may be dark, but his end shall be peace and everlasting light. A wicked man's way may be pleasant, but his end and abode for ever will be utter darkness.'[8]

Scripture is showing that a godly man may experience a condition of darkness of the soul that is not caused by sin. Such a saint feels emotionally bereft, while still in a state of obedience to God. It would appear that our Lord can allow us to suffer a state of darkness in order to increase our reliance on him. The message of Scripture is that we should trust our Lord not only when we feel uplifted, but also when we feel low. Note that the response to darkness of the soul is to trust in God. There is no place for psychotherapy.

(a) Sorrow of the soul

Scripture gives many examples of godly men who experienced sorrow of the soul. In *Lamentations* the prophet Jeremiah expresses profound misery because of the great disaster that has come upon Jerusalem. 'My eyes overflow with rivers of water for the destruction of the daughter of my people. My eyes flow and do not cease, without interruption, till the Lord from Heaven looks down and sees. My eyes bring suffering to my soul because of all the daughters of my city' *(Lamentations 3.48-51)*. Ezra was severely afflicted in his soul and mourned when he realised that the Israelites had mixed themselves with the people of the lands *(Ezra 9.2)*. Nehemiah was downcast when he learned that the wall of Jerusalem was broken down. 'So it was, when I heard these words, that I sat down and wept, and mourned for many days; I was fasting and praying before the God of heaven' *(Nehemiah 1.4)*. Paul speaks of his great sorrow and the continual grief in his heart because of his deep concern about the spiritual condition of his countrymen according to the flesh *(Romans 9.2-3)*.

The common theme of these examples is a deep sorrow of the soul experienced because of concern for the plight of God's people. God's servants saw the trouble caused by sin and they were deeply affected in their soul. In a similar way, we live in a fallen world in which we see the most heart-rending suffering caused by the blindness and godlessness of human behaviour; we see terrible natural disasters that occur in a creation subject to decay; we hear of the most appalling human suffering caused by man's inhumanity to man; we know of atrocities committed in the name of religion; we experience the suffering and sadness caused by disease, accidents and congenital abnormalities and 'we ourselves groan within ourselves' *(Romans 8.23)*.

(b) The discouragement of Elijah

We have the example of Elijah, who after his intense spiritual battle against the 450 prophets of Baal and the 400 prophets of Asherah, was afraid and ran for his life when he was threatened by wicked Jezebel. After a day's journey into the wilderness he sat down under a broom tree and prayed that he might die. 'It is enough! Now, Lord, take my life, for I am no better than my fathers!' *(1 Kings 19.3-4)*. (Many in the Christian counselling movement use this as an example of clinical depression.) We understand that even the most committed Christian may be prone to despair and discouragement in times of extreme fatigue or fear.

But God cared for his exhausted, fearful, discouraged prophet. An angel of the Lord touched Elijah, twice provided food and water and encouraged him to eat and drink. The prophet then journeyed for forty days and nights to the mountain of God at Horeb, where the word of the Lord came to him, 'What are you doing here, Elijah?' *(1 Kings 19.9)*. The prophet explained his frustration to the Lord: 'I have been very zealous for the Lord God of hosts; for the children of Israel have forsaken Your covenant, torn down Your altars and killed Your prophets with the sword. I alone am left; and they seek to take my life' (v10). Here we see the prophet's zeal for the Lord and his people. Having heard the prophet's heartfelt complaint, the Lord appeared to him in a still small voice.

The Lord re-commissioned the prophet by instructing him to anoint Hazael as king over Syria, Jehu as king over Israel and Elisha as prophet in his place. Faithful, courageous Elijah obeyed the Lord's instruction, and was later taken up into Heaven in a chariot of fire. To suggest, as the Christian counselling movement does, that Elijah was exhibiting the symptoms of clinical depression is nonsense. The lesson that we learn is that even the strongest of believers is prone to experience times of discouragement, and that we are often most vulnerable after a great spiritual victory. The response to spiritual discouragement is to listen to God's Word and to obey his commandments.

(c) A downcast soul

Psalms 42 and *43* give a clear description of spiritual despondency among God's people. The psalmist is in despair because he is far from the house of God. And so he asks the question: 'Why are you cast down, O my soul? And why are you disquieted within me?' *(Psalm 42.5)*. He is being reproached by his enemies with the continuous taunt, 'Where is your God?' In a moment of despair the psalmist feels abandoned by God – 'Why have You forgotten me? Why do I go mourning because of the oppression of the enemy?' *(Psalm 42.9)*. The psalmist turns to God in prayer. 'Oh, send out Your light and Your truth! Let them lead me; let them bring me to Your holy hill and to Your tabernacle. Then I will go to the altar of God, to God my exceeding joy . . . Hope in God; for I shall yet praise Him, the help of my countenance and my God' *(Psalm 43.3, 5)*.

Notice the response of the psalmist to his downcast soul. First, he comes to his senses and remembers the promises of the God whom he serves. He does not give in to his feeling of despair or engage in self-pity but rather takes himself in hand and wrestles through his despondency. He reminds himself of what he really knows about his God and acknowledges that his exceeding joy is in God *(Psalm 43.4)*.

Second, the psalmist challenges his emotions – 'Why are you cast down, O my soul?' – and decides that he should be led by the light and truth of God's Word, not by his emotions. When he remembers the past blessings and joys of serving God, he knows that he must hope in the living God, the God for whom his soul thirsts *(Psalm 42.2)*.

Third, having thought deeply and prayerfully about his situation, the psalmist comes to the understanding that God has not changed. Therefore, he will go to the altar of God to seek forgiveness and restore his relationship with the God in whom he trusts, so that he can again worship and praise the God he loves.

The message of Scripture is that the people of God frequently experience a downcast soul, sorrow of the heart and deep grief. The response of the believer is not to seek psychological counselling but to trust in the promises of God. In *Fearless Pilgrim*, Faith Cook records how John Bunyan, after a serious illness, felt a great cloud of darkness descend on his spirit. Gloomy and depressed, he became acutely conscious of his spiritual deadness. Then a passage from Scripture sprang to mind, 'Ye are come unto mount Sion, and unto the city of the living God, the heavenly Jerusalem, and to an innumerable company of angels . . . and to Jesus, the mediator of the new covenant' *(Hebrews 12.22, 24, AV)*. Joy flooded Bunyan's soul and he wrote: 'I could scarce lie in my bed for joy and peace and triumph through Christ.'[9]

(3) A soul downcast by sin

A fundamental biblical principle, vehemently denied by the psycho-secular view of depression, is that sin is the root cause of misery and despair. The greatest example of suffering in the Bible occurs in the Garden of Gethsemane when our Lord, before the Cross, began to be troubled and deeply distressed. His soul was exceedingly sorrowful, even to death *(Mark 14.33-34)*. Such was his agony of soul that his sweat became like great drops of blood *(Luke 22.44)*. The cause of this agony was the realisation that he who knew no sin would become sin for us *(2 Corinthians 5.21)*. The Lord laid on Christ the iniquity of us all. The Father bruised his Son and made his soul an offering for sin *(Isaiah 53.10)*. Christ knew that the consequences of bearing the sins of his people meant separation from God the Father, and this caused the Lord of Glory intense suffering. But he did not succumb – in his struggle our Lord prayed that the will of God be done.

Personal sin causes a troubled spirit, a guilty conscience, spiritual darkness and deep distress – what we have termed a *downcast soul*. The Lord warns Israel of the consequences of not obeying his laws. 'The Lord will give you a trembling heart, failing eyes, and anguish of soul. Your life shall hang in doubt before you; you shall fear day and night, and have no assurance of life. In the morning you shall say, "Oh, that it were evening!" And at evening you shall say, "Oh, that it were morning!" because of the fear which terrifies your heart, and because of the sight which your eyes see' *(Deuteronomy 28.65-67)*. The Lord warns Israel that if they do not obey all his commandments, he 'will even appoint terror over you, wasting disease and fever which shall consume the eyes and cause sorrow of heart' *(Leviticus 26.16)*. The Lord God, through the prophet Isaiah, twice says, 'There is no peace for the wicked' for the 'wicked are like the troubled sea, when it cannot rest, whose waters cast up mire and dirt' *(Isaiah 57.20-21)*. The way of the wicked is fraught with trouble and distress, for 'the perverse person is an abomination to the Lord . . . the curse of the Lord is on the house of the wicked' *(Proverbs 3.32, 33)*. The apostle Paul declares that God will render to 'those who are self-seeking and do not obey the truth, but obey unrighteousness – indignation and wrath, tribulation and anguish, on every soul of man who does evil' *(Romans 2.8-9)*.

There is no more desperate position than to be without God and without hope in this world. The man without God is walking according to the prince of the power of the air, the spirit who works in the sons of disobedience. His thinking is futile and his understanding is darkened, being alienated from the life of God because of the blindness of his heart *(Ephesians 4)*. His spiritual darkness, futile thinking and guilty conscience lead to unhappiness, misery and despair. Our experience confirms the truth of Scripture. Think for a moment of the misery, despair and suffering caused by adultery, abortion, divorce, illicit drugs, violence and murder, rape, sexual immorality, rebellious children, to mention only a few of the outward sins of man. And now think of the misery and suffering caused by envy, covetousness and lying. Yet sin does not always cause overt misery and suffering. Our Lord mentioned the rich fool who has many goods and takes his ease, with the philosophy of eat, drink, and be merry *(Luke 12.19)*.

(a) Downcast Cain

When Cain's offering was not accepted by the Lord, he was very angry and his face was downcast. The Lord told Cain that if he did right he would be accepted, but Cain ignored the Lord's warning and chose to murder his brother. He murdered Abel because his works were evil and his brother's righteous *(1 John 3.12)*. Cain experienced deep and profound agony as a direct consequence of his sin. God's judgement upon Cain included a curse that would make him a restless wanderer on the earth. In his despair, Cain responded, 'My punishment is greater than I can bear' *(Genesis 4.13)*. Cain's despair, manifest in the symptoms of fear, anger, and hopelessness, was a direct result of his own sin and his refusal to repent.

(b) King Saul's troubled spirit

King Saul is another example of sin and rebellion causing deep despair. He disobeyed the command of God by not completely destroying the Amalekites, preferring to be popular with his men. The prophet Samuel told Saul, 'Because you have rejected the word of the Lord, He also has rejected you from being king' *(1 Samuel 15.23)*. Because of his disobedience to God's commandments, God took the throne away from Saul, who fell into deep bouts of despair. 'The Spirit of the Lord departed from Saul, and a distressing spirit from the Lord troubled him' *(1 Samuel 16.14)*.

Envious of David's popularity with the people of Israel, Saul pursued David in order to kill him. Under a tamarisk tree in Ramah, with a spear in his hand, Saul said to his servants who stood about him, 'There is no one who reveals to me that my son has made a covenant with the son of Jesse; and there is not one of you who is *sorry for me* or reveals to me that my son has stirred up my servant against me . . .' *(1 Samuel 22.8)*. Full of self-pity, Saul ordered the execution of the priest Ahimelech, for he had given David holy bread. At Saul's command, Doeg the Edomite killed 85 priests of the Lord.

When Saul saw the army of the Philistines gathered together for battle he was afraid, and his heart troubled him greatly. Such was Saul's despair that he consulted a medium at Endor who called up Samuel. Saul told Samuel of his suffering, 'I am deeply distressed; for the Philistines make war against me, and God has departed from me and does not answer me anymore' *(1 Samuel 28.15)*. Saul's intense misery of soul was caused by his disobedience to God's commandments and his refusal to repent. Undoubtedly, a counsellor who followed the *psycho-secular* approach to mental illness would have diagnosed Saul as suffering from clinical depression. Scripture tells us that Saul was disobedient, self-serving and full of self-pity.

Depression among believers and unbelievers

The Christian counselling movement infers that when it comes to depression there is no difference in the experiences of believers and unbelievers. As we saw, Dr Mike Davies claims that because evangelical churches provide environments that are caring and supportive, individuals with mental health issues may be attracted to them. 'If this is so, it would follow that the incidence of mental ill health in our congregations may be greater than in the wider community.'[10] We are told that Christians suffer with depression just like everybody else. That is, faith in Christ does not affect our tendency to become depressed.

This claim is based on the assumption that depression is an established disease, like diabetes, and therefore it follows that Christians are expected to have an incidence similar to the rest of society. This view is now commonly believed and taught in evangelical churches.

However, Scripture draws a contrast between the many sorrows of the wicked and the joy of the upright in heart. 'Many sorrows shall be to the wicked; but he who trusts in the Lord, mercy shall surround him. Be glad in the Lord and rejoice, you righteous; and shout for joy, all you upright in heart' *(Psalm 32.10-11)*. As we have already seen, the fallen nature of man is behind all human suffering, fear, guilt and despair. Those who reject the Gospel of Christ are spiritually dead in their trespasses and sins, walking according to the course of this world and under the sway of the prince of darkness who works in the sons of disobedience. Unbelievers are by nature children of wrath, 'having no hope and without God in the world' *(Ephesians 2.12)*. In their hopeless state they frequently suffer despair, unhappiness and depression under the weight of their sin and unbelief.

Believers have been made spiritually alive in Christ and have been saved from the wrath to come through the mercy and grace of God. Having been justified by faith we have peace with God through our Lord Jesus Christ. He dwells in our heart through faith, and we know something of the love of Christ which passes knowledge. We know the joy of sins forgiven and fellowship with our heavenly Father. Through God working in our lives, we are being transformed into the image of Christ. With this knowledge we have joy unspeakable and our eternal hope is in Christ and the promises of God who will never leave us or forsake us. The apostle Paul encourages his fellow believers, whose names are in the Book of Life, to rejoice in the Lord always, and to be anxious about nothing, 'but in everything by prayer and supplication, with thanksgiving, let your requests be made known to God; and the peace of God, which surpasses all understanding, will guard your hearts and minds through Christ Jesus' *(Philippians 4.4-7)*.

Christ said to his disciples, 'Peace I leave with you, My peace I give to you; not as the world gives do I give to you. Let not your heart be troubled, neither let it be afraid' *(John 14.27)*. A feature of the Christian life is that believers can experience the joy of peace and thankfulness even in the trials and adverse circumstances that cause their sorrow and suffering.

The apostle Paul rejoiced in his sufferings for the church *(Colossians 1.24)*. He commends his ministry to the Corinthians by describing his great sufferings and tribulations for the sake of the Gospel, 'as sorrowful, yet always rejoicing' *(2 Corinthians 6.10)*. In his *Letter to the Romans*, Paul gives this encouragement – having been justified by faith we have access by faith into the grace of God, 'and rejoice in hope of the glory of God. And not only that, but we also glory in tribulations, knowing that tribulation produces perseverance; and perseverance, character; and character, hope' *(Romans 5.2-4)*.

Peter tells Christians to expect fiery trials which God allows to try them, 'but rejoice to the extent that you partake of Christ's sufferings' *(1 Peter 4.13)*. James exhorts his brothers in Christ to 'count it all joy when you fall into various trials, knowing that the testing of your faith produces patience' *(James 1.2-3)*. A Christian believer can know the joy of peace and thankfulness even in the worst suffering because he knows that God is faithful and good, and has promised that nothing in all creation, not tribulation, nor distress, nor persecution, nor famine, nor nakedness, nor peril, nor sword, is able to separate him from the love of God which is in Christ Jesus *(Romans 8.35-39)*. A great paradox of the Christian faith is that joy may be the outcome of suffering and sorrow for Christ's sake, since Christian joy is a gift of the Holy Spirit and comes from a deep trust in the nature and character of God.

While some Christians suffer often from walking in darkness and others less often, all Christians live in the joy of knowing Christ as their Saviour and Lord. The spirit of unbelief is fear, guilt, hopelessness and shame; those who live in unbelief are subject to misery and despair. The reason 'depression' is so common in many congregations is because they are made up of nominal Christians who are not born again. Those who say that the incidence of depression among Christians is the same as the world of unbelief have no understanding of the Gospel of salvation.

A problem for the Christian counselling movement is that having accepted without question the *psycho-secular* model of depression, it does not acknowledge the spiritual nature of depression. It follows that the counselling industry is unable to understand the real cause of the troubled spirit in their clients. What this means is that people with spiritual problems are being falsely labelled as mentally ill and provided with inappropriate psychotherapy and antidepressant drugs. The unbeliever is being turned away from the Cross, the hope of forgiveness and new birth in Christ, while the Christian believer is being encouraged to place his faith in a false hope that is built on the wisdom of men, and is foolishness in God's eyes.

Responding to a downcast soul

How should a Christian respond to deep despair, a downcast soul, a grieving heart? Scripture is clear that a believer should respond by trusting the promises of God. Contrary to what the Christian counselling movement says, a true believer will turn to the Word of God for his comfort and encouragement, for 'the Lord is good to those who wait for Him, to the soul who seeks Him. It is good that one should hope and wait quietly for the salvation of the Lord' *(Lamentations 3.25-26)*.

Those who are suffering because of sin need to confess and repent, following the example of David in *Psalm 51*.

Those who are suffering because of adverse circumstances need to cleave to the God of all comfort in their time of trouble, with the assurance that 'all things work together for good to those who love God, to those who are the called according to His purpose' *(Romans 8.28)*. They need encouragement and support that comes from fellowship with other believers. They do what is right and best for their hearts and souls by remaining faithful in their service for the Lord, continuing to draw daily help from the Bible, praying earnestly to God, and believing his numerous, glorious promises. All Christians are indwelt by the Holy Spirit and we must look to him for strength to obey God's commands. Paul prays to the Father that believers 'be strengthened with might through His Spirit in the inner man . . .' *(Ephesians 3.16)*. Those who are downcast by the pressures of life should take encouragement from *Psalms 42* and *43*.

As believers we have a great High Priest, Jesus the Son of God, who knows and sympathises with our weaknesses and struggles, for in his human nature he was in all points tempted like we are, yet without sin. Our Saviour suffers with us, for he has experienced our emotional pain and he understands our needs. Therefore, in our time of deepest need, we can confidently come to the throne of grace, to our heavenly Father, for it is there that we find mercy and grace to help us overcome our weaknesses and despair and to meet our needs *(Hebrews 4.14-16)*.

It is imperative for the church to do all it can to support believers who are living in despair. Other believers (not secular therapists) should come alongside their downcast brother or sister to offer comfort and spiritual encouragement, and even to read the Scriptures and pray together. The loss of sharing one another's burdens, of hospitality, of coming alongside in mutual encouragement in times of trouble has been one of the great tragedies of the psychological onslaught. Instead of helping our fellow believers many churches are sending downcast Christians to a counsellor.

In *The Pilgrim's Progress* the two pilgrims, Christian and Hopeful, were finding the Way rough and their feet were aching. When they came to a delightful meadow that lay next to the Way, the temptation was great. Christian said, 'Here is the easiest going; come Hopeful, and let us go over.' Hopeful, however, was concerned, 'But how if this path should lead us out of the Way?' Despite Hopeful's misgivings, the two pilgrims decided to cross the stile into the meadow, where the going was much easier.

But when night came it grew very dark and began to rain and thunder in a very dreadful manner. Hopeful groaned, 'Oh that I had kept on my Way!' Then Giant Despair confronted the pilgrims for trespassing on his land and forced them to Doubting Castle, where they were thrown into 'a very dark dungeon, nasty and stinking to the spirit of these two men . . . Now in this place Christian had double sorrow, because 'twas through his unadvised haste that they were brought into this distress.' On the advice of his wife, Giant Despair beat the pilgrims fearfully and then left them to mourn their distress with sighs and bitter lamentations. The Giant told them that because they were unlikely to escape they should make an end of themselves. Christian lamented, 'The life that we now live is miserable, for my part, I know not whether is best to live thus or to die out of hand?'

In the depths of despair, the pilgrims began to pray. It was then that Christian came to his senses. 'What a fool am I, thus to lie in a stinking dungeon, when I may as well walk at liberty. I have a key in my bosom, called promise, that will (I am persuaded) open any lock in Doubting Castle. And so, trusting in the promises of God, the dungeon door flew open with ease, and Christian and Hopeful came out and returned to the Way.'

Bunyan is showing that Christians who leave the Way, through sin and disobedience, will suffer the torments of despair. The answer is to trust in the promises of God, and return to the Way. We should remember that sometimes it takes a longer time to overcome our despair than Bunyan suggests in *The Pilgrim's Progress*.

Conclusion

We have identified two views of depression that are fundamentally opposed to each other – the *psycho-secular disease* model of depression that has been constructed by the *DSM*, the bible of psychiatry, from its stance in secular humanism, and the *biblical* view which is based on the wisdom of Scripture. According to the *psycho-secular* view, people with a label of depression are ill and in need of treatment with antidepressant drugs and psychotherapy. The Christian counselling movement has simply accepted the *psycho-secular* disease model of depression at face value and is promoting it in the churches. As a result many Christians are being given a diagnosis of clinical depression and deceived into believing that antidepressant drugs and cognitive therapy are the answer for their troubled souls.

According to the biblical view, deep despair, walking in darkness and a downcast soul are most often 'ordinary' spiritual conditions, and the answer is always to trust the promises of God. It is the duty of God's people to come alongside their fellow believers in their time of trouble and despair; to admonish, to support, to care for and mutually encourage one another.

In *Psalm 143* David records how persecution had brought his soul very low: 'He has crushed my life to the ground; he has made me dwell in darkness, like those who have long been dead. Therefore my spirit is overwhelmed within me; my heart within me is distressed' (vv3-4). His remedy was to meditate on God's past goodness to him: 'I meditate on all Your works; I muse on the work of Your hands. I spread out my hands to You; my soul longs for You like a thirsty land. Answer me speedily, O Lord; my spirit fails! Do not hide Your face from me, lest I be like those who go down into the pit. Cause me to hear Your loving-kindness in the morning, for in You do I trust; cause me to know the way in which I should walk, for I lift my soul to You' (vv5-8).

The lifting up of downcast believers is the task of biblical ministry, but the adoption of secular therapies is wresting God's people away from the only true and effective relief for their souls. The next chapters will show the kind of false remedies now replacing scriptural comfort.

4
The Theory of Unconditional Love

THE IDEA of unconditional love has now gained wide acceptance among Christians and is frequently referred to from pulpits and in Christian books. Joyce Meyer, the well-known TV evangelist, explains the power of God's unconditional love in this manner: 'The only way to overcome feelings of worthlessness is by receiving God's unconditional love. We cannot properly love ourselves, or others, until we receive this. Money, power, fame . . . nothing besides God can satisfy our deep desire to be loved and accepted. All you have to do is open your heart and make the decision to receive God's love.'[1]

It must be said that many people use the term unconditional love innocently, when they wish to speak of long-suffering love. They do not realise that this term strictly refers to an anti-biblical notion of love.

Philip Yancey, editor-at-large for *Christianity Today* and prolific award-winning author, writes, 'Only Christianity dares to make God's love unconditional.'[2] Author of *The Purpose Driven Life*, Rick Warren writes, 'You will never understand how much God loves you here on earth. There is nothing you can ever do in life that will make God love you more than he already does. There is nothing you can ever do that will make God love you any less. His love is not based on your performance. It's unconditional love. It's based on who he is.'[3]

Unconditional love is one of the cornerstones of the emerging church movement. Steve Chalke, founder of Faithworks and leader of the emerging church in the UK, believes that if we sit back and just wait for people to flock to our churches we will have a long wait. 'We need to be getting out, getting our hands dirty and helping people where they are at. We need to show the unconditional love of Jesus to our society that increasingly doesn't know him. We have to show that we care.'[4] In *The Lost Message of Jesus* (2005) Chalke says a child should know 'Jesus explained that God loves them unconditionally.'[5] In response to a letter criticising him for overemphasising God's love, Chalke's defence was straightforward: 'How can I ever find words to describe God's unconditional love let alone overemphasise the thing?'[6]

In *An Emerging Church Primer* Justin Taylor writes, 'The core Christian message is unchanged but emerging churches attempt, as the church has throughout the centuries, to find ways to reach God's people where they are to hear God's message of unconditional love.'[7]

Jay Bakker, founder of Revolutionary Ministries, states that his goal is to 'show all people the unconditional love and grace of Jesus without any reservations due to their lifestyle or religious background, past or future'. And all means all. Bakker is clear that he could not compromise by excluding gay people or any other group.[8]

A group of Christian clergy, who believe that homosexuality is a good gift of God, wrote: 'We are Christian Clergy grounded in the witness of the Bible and convicted of the unconditional love of God for all people. We have come together to raise a voice against the Christian intolerance that promotes condemnation, discrimination, and hatred towards gays, lesbians, bisexuals, and transgendered persons.'[9]

Christians involved in crisis pregnancy counselling claim to be motivated by unconditional Christian love. A major counselling centre explains that its counsellors offer free, confidential, non-directive counselling to women who are considering abortion. They provide a listening ear, accurate information and friendly, non-judgemental support.[10] 'The aim is not to tell people how to proceed, but to explain carefully what abortion means and provide information about the other options (carrying the baby to term and then either keeping it or offering it for adoption). Ongoing care [is available] for those who decide to proceed with abortion with full post-abortion counselling. Motivated by *unconditional* Christian love, we will aim to provide much needed care for the women concerned.'[11]

What is interesting about this example is that unconditional Christian love is seen as expressing itself through non-judgemental, non-directive counselling. Unconditional love means here that you will not say abortion is wrong. Clearly this form of counselling follows Carl Rogers' model of counselling rather than biblical truth.

It is helpful to know that attaching the word 'unconditional' to God's love is a relatively recent phenomenon. Over the last few decades it has silently slipped into the evangelical vocabulary and gained a solid foothold in Christian thinking. Such is the acceptance of unconditional love that it is now regarded by many as part of orthodox Christian doctrine. As Christians we are encouraged to spread the message of God's unconditional love. Because God loves us unconditionally we must love others in the same way. The author of *The Purpose Driven Life*, Rick Warren, says Christians should offer unconditional love to people with AIDS instead of faulting them for how they may have caught the disease.[12]

Christian counselling promotes unconditional love

The Christian counselling movement particularly is given over to the concept of unconditional love. We would be hard pressed to find a Christian counsellor who does not promote the idea. In *Effective Biblical Counselling* Larry Crabb stresses the importance of unconditional love. 'My need for security demands that I be unconditionally loved, accepted and cared for, now and forever. God has seen me at my worst and still loved me to the point of giving his life for me. That kind of love I can never lose. I am completely acceptable to him regardless of my behaviour.'[13]

Selwyn Hughes claims that an essential requirement of the human soul is to be loved unconditionally. 'We will never resolve the identity crisis in our souls until we know how to relate to the true God who alone can give us what our souls require – unconditional love and eternal meaning.'[14] Hughes goes on to explain that God loved Adam and Eve unconditionally. 'Adam and Eve, because of their close and intimate relationship with God, knew what it meant to be unconditionally loved, highly valued, and for their lives to have total meaning. They would have felt secure, worthwhile and significant.'[15]

Hughes teaches that the Fall has caused an identity crisis for human beings. Our deep psychological longings for security, self-worth and significance have suffered a severe blow that has caused us to become insecure, to feel inferior and insignificant. The answer, in Hughes' mind, is unconditional love. 'Identity depends on three things – a sense that one is unconditionally loved, a sense of one's value, and a sense of meaning and purpose . . . By security I mean the positive feelings that flood the soul when we know that we are loved and loved unconditionally . . . The more aware I am that God loves me – and loves me unconditionally – the easier it is for me to do my tasks and relate well to others.'[16]

What we need, says Hughes, is a sense that God loves us unconditionally so that we feel better about ourselves, so that we feel secure and significant and have healthy self-esteem. However, this psychological view of the Fall ignores the holiness of God and fails to acknowledge the sinfulness of mankind. What Hughes portrays is a permissive God who makes us feel good about ourselves, no matter what. Scripture, however, describes the Fall not as a psychological disaster but as man's rebellion against his Creator. Mankind does not have an identity crisis but a problem with sin.

David Seamands teaches that the two major causes of most emotional problems among evangelical Christians are the failure to understand and live out God's unconditional grace and forgiveness, and the failure to give out that unconditional love, forgiveness, and grace to other people.[17] According to Seamands the failure of Christians to grasp the amazing fact that God's grace, love and forgiveness is unconditional leads to emotional problems and inner pain. The result is that emotionally hurting Christians are unable to give out unconditional love and forgiveness. Seamands believes that when evangelical Christians come to understand the dogma of unconditional love most of their emotional problems will be solved.

Dr Charles Stanley, the senior pastor of the First Baptist Church of Atlanta and a past president of the Southern Baptist Convention, explains the power of unconditional love from *Colossians 3.21*. 'Expressing unconditional love empowers parents to raise kids to be confident adults. By accepting each child's unique nature, we lay a foundation for good self-esteem. Too often we unintentionally inflict damage on a young one's ego by confusing actions with personhood – a child might hear criticism as "I'm bad" rather than "my behaviour was wrong." Children desperately need parental guidance and discipline, but these must be wrapped in actions and language that convey love. The alternative – correcting a child with the aim of making him or her the adult Mom or Dad desires instead of the person God intends – promotes a rebellious spirit . . . The result of unconditional love and its by-products – self-esteem and obedience – is that children develop good relationships.'[18]

Unconditional love is an important tenet of marriage counselling, as we shall see in chapter 9. Marriage counsellor Dr Gary Chapman, in *The Five Love Languages, Singles Edition* (2009), asserts that 'everyone has a God-given desire for complete and unconditional love in all relationships'.[19] James Dobson says: 'I endeavoured to sum up the importance of selfless, unconditional love in my book *Love for a Lifetime*.'[20] Marriage counsellors Gary Smalley and John Trent teach that the unconditional love and approval that comes with God's blessing is an important element of our self-esteem and emotional well-being.[21]

Is unconditional love biblical?

So where does the idea of *unconditional* love come from? Older Christians will know that it was not taught when they were young people. Moreover no serious Christian theologian has used the term. We will search in vain to find the term 'unconditional love' in the great Christian doctrinal writings of the past, or in books on systematic theology. And this is not surprising for Scripture does not refer to God's love as unconditional. So where does the term come from?

Erik Fromm was one of the first to use the phrase 'unconditional love'. As a psychologist he was impressed by the apparent happiness and security of children in a Mexican orphanage and put it down to the unconditional love that the children experienced from the staff. He identified a basic condition that every child needs, 'the principle of unconditional motherly love. A mother loves her child unconditionally. If mothers loved their children only because they performed well, most infants would die.'[22] Fromm described a father's love for his children as conditional and assumed that mothers have unconditional love. Carl Rogers coined the phrase 'unconditional positive regard', by which he meant the granting of love and approval regardless of an individual's behaviour.

Unconditional love and the New Age movement

The dogma of unconditional love has been readily accepted and promoted by many secular groups and organisations. It is also widely promoted by the New Age movement and by a number of pagan organisations. Harold W. Becker, a New Age devotee, has dedicated his life to promoting the concept of unconditional love. His book *Unconditional Love – An Unlimited Way of Being* (2007) explains that one by one, people around the world are awakening to an energy and power that is transforming the course of all humanity. 'An inner impulse is driving us forward and asking us to evolve beyond our current reality. This silent force promises to change forever the way we live on this planet. We, as a race of people, are becoming consciously aware of unconditional love. The greatest power known to man is that of unconditional love . . .'[23] Becker says that religions have flourished and perished while claiming the path to love. 'We, the people of this planet, may have missed the simplicity of unconditional love. Trying to seek love through an outer process, we ignore its true residence. The power of unconditional love is within each of us. Anchored within our hearts is the opportunity to expand our reality. We need only turn our attention to the inner feelings of love and cultivate its expression to reap infinite rewards.'[24]

Becker believes that the power of love is permeating everywhere and again claiming our hearts. 'In truth, we are recalling our divinity. We remember we are spiritual beings having a human experience. We no longer need to search for some higher nature outside ourselves: we are the higher power when we come from unconditional love.'[25]

Roy Klienwachter, an ordained minister and author of New Age Wisdom books, in a carefully argued article explains the meaning of unconditional love. 'Unconditional love means unconditional freedom. Love and freedom are two of those words that are interchangeable. Freedom of choice is unconditional love, unconditional freedom. Choice is another of those words that are interchangeable with love and freedom. For the most part humanity understands little of what the word unconditional means. Unconditional means . . . no conditions. This lack of understanding is what has divided man from man and religion from religion throughout his sojourn in the physical reality. It is again man's ego trying to grasp the idea, and not being able to surrender to its meaning. Let me demonstrate. The one common thread that I have found weaving through man's many belief systems is: God is Unconditional Love. I have yet to have anyone tell me that this is not so. It seems to be accepted by all belief systems that are centred around a creator.'[26]

Klienwachter explains that unconditional means that there are no conditions to God's love. If there was a condition to God's love, then God would be giving conditional love. And freedom is given from unconditional love. Because love, freedom and choice are unconditional, there can be no punishment. This point is emphasised. 'Here is where the so-called enlightened fall by the wayside. They cannot accept any of these things without the recourse of punishment. You can practise unconditional love, unconditional freedom and unconditional choice with no punishments! God will never punish you! Retribution is a lie, it was all made up. Only man will punish you. Anyone who tells you different, is not coming from unconditional love. They live in fear of you practising these things. They do not understand what unconditional means.' [27]

Buddhism and unconditional love

The definition of love in Buddhism is wanting others to be happy. This love is unconditional and it requires a lot of courage and acceptance including self-acceptance. Conditional love or selfish love is the 'near enemy' of love, a quality which appears similar, but is actually more an opposite.[28]

A Buddhist priest explains the concept of unconditional love. 'In the Metta Sutra, on the subject of Love, the Buddha took the strongest of all possible positions: that everything that is alive deserves Love every moment of every day, no matter what . . . That was the nature of the Love he was inviting us to encounter: Unconditional. And that is a key to the powerful effects it has on the mind.

'We can understand the effects this kind of Love has by thinking about what it is like to be in the presence of a person who accepts us as we are, unconditionally. Whether we're too heavy or too thin, too loud or too quiet. No matter how we look that day. Even if we're in a lousy mood – this person loves and accepts us exactly as we are. We don't need to worry about losing their love if we fail to meet some standard that day. Because their love isn't based on something we do or don't do. It's something much deeper. It's unconditional.'[29]

In their book *Unconditional Love*, Eddie and Debbie Shapiro discuss the paths of Buddhism and yoga. They explain that 'true happiness can only be attained through a connection to our spiritual heart. Unconditional love asks that we look into ourselves and go beyond the ego to find deeper levels of loving kindness, forgiveness and tolerance. Uplifting and inspiring, it compels the reader to live with integrity, fearlessness and the vastness of an integrated heart.'[30]

Unconditional love and the occult

Aleister Crowley was a man who gave himself to the occult. He founded a mystical and religious system named Thelema and was a preacher of unconditional love. His system was based on the two ideals: 'Do what thou wilt shall be the whole of the law' and 'Love is the law, love under will.'[31] Crowley taught that the law is an invitation to do as you want with no controlling demands or conditions, but to love and accept others unconditionally, allowing them to live by their personal truths. In addressing a jury, Mr Justice Swift said of Crowley, 'I have never heard such dreadful, horrible, blasphemous and abominable stuff as that which has been produced by the man [Crowley] who describes himself to you as the greatest living poet.'[32]

The Voice of Lucifer website declares in bold type – 'Help us to save our world. Love yourselves unconditionally. Share this unconditional love with everyone, friends and foes alike. In a world beset by hate on all sides, it is incumbent upon Luciferians to balance this hatred with unconditional love. We believe that love is our only hope.' The website explains that unconditional love is the greatest power known to man.

The website continues, 'Simply stated, unconditional love is an unlimited way of being. We are without any limit to our thoughts and feelings in life and can create any reality we choose to focus our attention upon. There are infinite imaginative possibilities when we allow the freedom to go beyond our perceived limits. If we can dream it, we can build it. Life, through unconditional love, is a wondrous adventure that excites the very core of our being and lights our path with delight.'

Luciferians 'preach unconditional love as a way of changing our world for the better. It is the only thing that can save us from experiencing a world of hatred, ignorance and war. We are the creators of our experiences. We are the architects of our universe. We are responsible for our own redemption. Unconditional love is the sole vehicle for our salvation and the preservation of our species and planet. Luciferians therefore preach unconditional love as the way of changing our world for the better.'[33]

Conclusion

Clearly the concept of unconditional love is held in common by the emerging church movement, the Christian counselling movement, New Age thinking, Eastern religions and Luciferians. It is not difficult to see that the permissive nature of unconditional love is very different from the nature of God's redeeming love described in Scripture.

The concept of unconditional love only exists in a mythological world in which there is no sin, no evil and no law, in which people are free to live as they like without fear of judgement and punishment. In the real world, unconditional love is no more and no less than licentiousness – an attitude that denies the accepted rules and morals that govern human behaviour. It is an attitude that allows us to do what we want without sanction or control. It is the essential message of pagan morality and New Age salvation.

5
The Fallacy of Unconditional Love

IS UNCONDITIONAL LOVE a biblical concept? As we saw in the previous chapter, it is a concept shared by Christian counsellors, secular psychologists, New Age adherents, Buddhists and Luciferians, among others. The Bible does not mention the term and no serious theologian describes God's love as unconditional. We must conclude, therefore, that it is not a biblical concept but a construct from the imagination of man. The basic premise is that God loves all human beings exactly as they are, no matter how they behave. Larry Crabb explains, 'I am completely acceptable to him regardless of my behaviour.'[1] That is, no matter how a person acts, God's unconditional love means that person is acceptable to God.

We have seen that unconditional love is closely related to the idea of self-esteem. While self-esteem attempts to make man feel good about his sin, unconditional love attempts to make sinful man feel that he will not face judgement or punishment. Both are counterfeits, for they deny that we live in a fallen world controlled by sin and evil. The basic premise of unconditional love is that we live in a lawless world. Therefore we are free to live as we like, to do what we want, and we will not be judged, condemned or punished. No matter how we behave, we are acceptable to the god of unconditional love. So exactly who is the god of unconditional love?

The amoral world of unconditional love

In the previous chapter we saw the claim by Selwyn Hughes that God loved Adam and Eve unconditionally. The Fall is interpreted as a psychological disaster which made man feel insecure, inferior and insignificant. Is this a proper interpretation of Scripture? Or is Scripture being misused to support the dogma of unconditional love?

At the time of creation the Lord God saw that everything he had made was very good. Man created in the image of God was a responsible, moral human being who was able to distinguish right from wrong, and capable of having a spiritual relationship with his Creator. When God placed the man in the Garden to work it, he set a moral test of Adam's obedience. The tree of life was in the middle of the Garden, and also the tree of the knowledge of good and evil. God told Adam that he could freely eat of every tree of the Garden, but of the tree of the knowledge of good and evil he should not eat *(Genesis 2.16-17)*. By this test Adam, who had a free will, could choose to show his love for the Lord God by obeying his command. God demonstrated his love by providing Adam with everything he could possibly need – he was given permission to freely eat of every tree, except for the one that God had forbidden. *Adam's continuing relationship with his Creator was conditional on his obedience to God's word.*

When Adam and Eve, who were representatives of the human race, ate the forbidden fruit they broke the divine condition – obedience to God's word – for an ongoing spiritual relationship. The consequence of disobeying God's command (condition) was that they were driven from the Garden of Eden and God's presence, and God placed cherubim, representing his holiness, and a flaming sword, representing his justice, to guard the way to the tree of life *(Genesis 3.24)*. Adam and Eve, and through them all mankind, became spiritually dead, not only separated from the love of God, but under the wrath of God. But God, who is rich in mercy, had a plan of salvation that would redeem man from his bondage to sin. The relationship with God, lost in the Garden of Eden, can only be restored by the Son of God whose heel was bruised on the cross of Calvary *(Genesis 3.15)*. Reconciliation with a holy God is conditional on faith in the blood of Christ which cleanses from all sin. Clearly, God's relationship with Adam and Eve in the Garden was conditional on them obeying his word, and this they failed to do.

The Christian counselling movement must answer these questions – if God loved Adam and Eve unconditionally why did he expel them from the Garden of Eden? Why did he not offer them unconditional forgiveness when they rebelled against his commandment? The answer, of course, is because the God of Scripture is a holy God who cannot tolerate sin. 'Exalt the Lord our God, and worship at His holy hill; for the Lord our God is holy' *(Psalm 99.9)*.

Those who promote the dogma of unconditional love demand a Garden of Eden without the tree of the knowledge of good and evil. They imagine a god who does not set man a moral standard by which he should live. They visualise a god who does not demand obedience. They picture a god who does not care what man does, how he behaves. In other words, they seek an amoral world, where man is king and God allows man to do whatever he pleases. This god would love man unconditionally, no matter what he did, no matter how he behaved, no matter how he treated others, even if he chose to kill, steal and destroy. This god would not judge wickedness, or punish wrongdoing. But such a god is amoral and wicked.

The God of the Bible, by stark contrast, is a holy God who demands obedience to his righteous Word. He is a just God who will judge the world according to his moral law. He is a righteous God who will punish sin and evil. The relationship between God and man is conditional on man obeying the Word of God. When Adam disobeyed God, he died spiritually and the relationship was broken – Adam hid from God. Yet God, in his *redeeming* love, had a plan to save man from his sin and to restore his relationship with a holy God. (Our Saviour was perfectly obedient to the Father and perfectly kept his holy, righteous law. Those in Christ, vicariously share Christ's perfect obedience.)

God's common grace and God's redeeming love

To understand what Scripture teaches about God's love, we need to distinguish between God's common grace and God's redeeming love. Common grace is extended to all that God has made. He makes his sun rise on the evil and sends rain on the just and the unjust *(Matthew 5.45)* and gives good gifts to all men. 'The Lord is good to all, and His tender mercies are over all His works . . . You open Your hand and satisfy the desire of every living thing' *(Psalm 145.9, 16)*. The Lord Jesus said of the Most High God, 'For He is kind to the unthankful and evil' *(Luke 6.35)*. The righteous judgement of God will render to each one according to his deeds: eternal life to those who, in Christ, patiently continue in doing good, but to those who are self-seeking and do not obey the truth, but obey unrighteousness – indignation and wrath *(Romans 2.6-8)*.

But not all men experience God's redeeming love: only those who through God's grace are quickened by the Holy Spirit and receive Christ by faith as their Saviour and Lord. The wonder of God's redeeming love is described in *Ephesians 1*. God chose the elect in Christ before the foundation of the world that we should be holy and without blame before him in love, having predestined us to adoption as sons by Jesus Christ to himself, according to the good pleasure of his will. In Christ we have redemption through his blood, the forgiveness of sins, according to the riches of his grace *(Ephesians 1.4-7)*.

So God's redeeming love is made manifest through the Cross of Christ. This is love – that Christ loved us and gave himself for us. 'By this we know love, because He laid down His life for us' *(1 John 3.16)*. God's redeeming love is consistent with his holy character and his moral law.

An essential aspect of God's character is that he is too holy to look upon sin. His love is expressed in his perfect moral law, which is the manifestation of his righteous, compassionate, holy character. According to Paul, love 'thinks no evil; does not rejoice in iniquity, but rejoices in the truth' *(1 Corinthians 13.5-6)*. God hates evil with an awesome intensity. Christ died for our sin because the holy God of the Bible cannot just overlook sin. God's justice demands that sin must be punished. God is love and light; and in him there is no darkness at all *(1 John 1.5)*.

The purpose of God's redeeming love is to reconcile God and man, to save lost sinners from the wrath of God's righteous judgement. 'In this the love of God was manifested toward us, that God has sent His only begotten Son into the world, that we might live through Him' *(1 John 4.9)*. 'God demonstrates His own love toward us, in that while we were still sinners, Christ died for us' *(Romans 5.8)*. Those who have been justified by the blood of Christ are reconciled to God and saved from the wrath of God *(Romans 5.9)*. God redeems Christian people, not to meet our psychological needs, but that we should be holy and without blame before him *(Ephesians 1.4)*. And the promise is that nothing in all creation is able to separate the true believer from the immeasurable love of God that is in Christ Jesus our Lord *(Romans 8.39)*. Only those who have experienced the saving power of Christ can understand the doctrine of God's redeeming love.

'For God so loved the world'

An examination of a well-known section of the third chapter of *John's Gospel* shows the true meaning of God's love as taught by his Word, and will also show the falseness of the dogma of unconditional love.

'For God so loved the world that He gave His only begotten Son, that whosoever believes in Him [God's condition] should not perish but have everlasting life [God's redeeming love in Christ]. For God did not send His Son into the world to condemn the world, but that the world through Him [God's condition] might be saved [God's redeeming love]. He who believes in Him [God's condition] is not condemned; but he who does not believe is condemned already [God's wrath and judgement], because he has not believed in the name of the only Son of God' *(John 3.16-18)*.

This passage places God's love in a proper context. God's love is revealed in his Son Jesus Christ. Because of his compassionate, merciful nature, God, who is holy, righteous and just, gave his Son to die for our sin. Salvation from sin is dependent on the Cross. Those who repent of their sins and put their faith in Christ are saved from God's wrath; those who do not believe face God's wrath and judgement. Any other teaching is false.

Love, obedience and discipline

An essential characteristic of God's people, saved by God's grace, is that they are obedient to God's law. They seek to walk in the way of God and to obey God's commandments. 'For this is the love of God, that we keep His commandments. And His commandments are not burdensome' *(1 John 5.3)*. Those who flout God's law are not true believers. The Lord made this abundantly clear when he said that those who love him are those who obey his commandments. 'If you love Me, keep My commandments ... He who has My commandments and keeps them, it is he who loves Me. And he who loves Me will be loved . by My Father, and I will love him and manifest Myself to him' *(John 14.15, 21)*.

An important aspect of God's love is that he disciplines his children. 'For whom the Lord loves He chastens, and scourges every son whom He receives' *(Hebrews 12.6)*. God disciplines his children for their own good, that they may share in his holiness *(Hebrews 12.10)*. Sometimes discipline can appear harsh at the time, but in the long run it produces a harvest of good works. Without discipline a child becomes unruly and wilful. The Bible instructs the father who loves his children to discipline them and to use the rod of correction when necessary.

The popular secular concept of unconditional love knows nothing of discipline. Indeed, any attempt at discipline, at correction or rebuke for wrongdoing, is seen to be unloving, judgemental and harsh. The world's promoters of unconditional love despise discipline for they want the freedom to do what they like without any restraint.

Counterfeit love

We should not be surprised that the master of lies, the great deceiver, Satan, has produced a counterfeit version of God's love for the church. To put the two words 'love' and 'unconditional' together is actually a contradiction in terms. How do we know that it is counterfeit? Because it denies the character of God and is, therefore, amoral. The premise on which the doctrine of 'unconditional love' is based is that God does not mind how a person behaves. So how can Larry Crabb say, 'I am completely acceptable to him regardless of my behaviour'? This would mean that you may do what you like, for God loves you unconditionally. You would be free to satisfy all your lustful passions, to lie, steal and cheat, and it would not matter for God loves you unconditionally. You may dishonour your parents, behave in a way that is faithless, heartless and ruthless, and it would not matter, because God loves you unconditionally. This is a deceptive term, because Scripture warns in the first chapter of *Romans* that those who give themselves to wilful wickedness and godlessness are without excuse and face God's judgement.

By contrast, God's love demands justice and the punishment of evil. The Cross of Christ is where the love of God and the justice of God meet. Christ, who was without sin, has paid the price of sin; he has borne God's judgement for sin. The people of God rejoice in the justice of God, for it is right that the wicked are punished for their sin. On the day of the Lord, God's righteous judgement will be revealed and he will give to each person according to what he has done. To those with an unrepentant heart, who reject the Truth and follow evil, there will be wrath and anger *(Romans 2.6-8)*. All who sin under the law will be judged by God's law. For wickedness not to be judged is the height of immorality. Yet the essence of unconditional love is non-judgementalism – the view that there is no day of judgement and no punishment for sin.

The principle of unconditional love requires God to love all people equally, even those who hate him, despise him, ignore his Word and mock his law. But this is a false view of God and his love. Does God's redeeming love extend to those who have wilfully rejected the Cross of Christ? Certainly not. Scripture warns that the wrath of God comes upon the sons of disobedience *(Ephesians 5.6)*. The psalmist tells us the God of Heaven holds in derision those who set themselves against the Lord and against his Anointed. Scripture warns us to serve the Lord with fear. 'Kiss the Son, lest He be angry, and you perish in the way, when His wrath is kindled but a little' *(Psalm 2.12)*. So what is the position of those who are dead in their trespasses and sins and have rejected God's Messiah? The Scriptures teach that they are under the wrath of God.

So where does the message of unconditional love come from? We have already seen that the New Age movement and the Voice of Lucifer are promoting 'unconditional love' as a central tenet of their faith. There is a god who claims to love unconditionally, and that is Lucifer, the god of this world. This is not genuine love, but the opposite of God's love. Although Satan can appear as an angel of light, he is a roaring lion seeking those he may devour. His purpose is to kill, steal and destroy.

The 'unconditional love' of the New Age movement is, in truth, the gateway to lawlessness, licentiousness and lust. It is a permissive idea that encourages people to do what they want, to live how they like, to disregard the God of the Bible. It is a message that suggests that there is no moral law and no eternal judgement. Those who follow it are in serious spiritual danger, for they have been deceived by the god of this age.

Incompatible with Christianity

What are we to make of Christians who teach 'unconditional love'? Undoubtedly many have been deceived by the god of this age, and carelessly teach wrong doctrine. They are mistaken because they have been enticed away from following God's Word. Others teach unconditional love because they are false teachers, committed to introducing strange doctrines into the household of God. They have traduced the message of God's love and distorted the Gospel of grace. Theirs is a false message, for it does not teach God's holiness and justice, or the glory of God's redeeming love, the essential nature of repentance and the joy of sins forgiven.

6
The Theory of Therapeutic Forgiveness

T HE IDEA of unconditional love is closely related to the concept of unconditional forgiveness. In chapter 4 we heard the claim that the failure of Christians to grasp the amazing fact that God's love and forgiveness is *unconditional* leads to emotional problems and inner pain.[1] It is now widely believed that Christians should forgive all who offend against them. The idea of unconditional forgiveness, encouraged by the Christian counselling movement, has almost become part of the Christian faith. Those who do not express total forgiveness are seen to be harbouring bitterness in their hearts. Unconditional forgiveness, or total forgiveness, is promoted as a therapeutic act that helps Christians to achieve inner healing.

When an ordained priest, the Rev Julie Nicholson, lost her daughter in the London bombings she decided to resign her post as she felt unable to forgive the bombers. She expressed her feelings about the outrageous murder: 'I rage that a human being could choose to take another human's life. I rage that someone should do this in the name of a God. I find that utterly offensive.'[2] (So does the God of Heaven.) She felt unable 'to celebrate the Eucharist, centred around peace, reconciliation and forgiveness as it is, when I feel so far from those things myself.'

In an article about the incident, Christian commentator Anne Atkins writes, '*Christianity demands forgiveness.* Repeatedly Jesus teaches us that if we want to be forgiven, we must first forgive. Mrs Nicholson finds herself unable to do this, and if she can't live out the message, she believes she must lay aside the ministry . . . Now I find myself with more questions about forgiveness than I can answer. Years ago I heard the superb preacher John Stott say there is no Christian forgiveness without repentance. I have long thought this inconsistent with a prayer to be forgiven as we forgive others – and surely a disastrous recipe for mental health: only I am the victim of my failure to forgive.'[3] (My italics.)

In evangelical circles it is expected that Christians should forgive everyone who wrongs them, and even forgive the most horrendous crimes. We hear of Christian parents whose child has been murdered declare that they have forgiven the murderer. The mother of Anthony Walker drew on her Christian faith to find forgiveness for the two thugs who murdered her son with a mountaineering axe because he was black. After two young men were found guilty of the murder Mrs Walker is reported to have said: 'Do I forgive them? At the point of death Jesus said, "I forgive them because they don't know what they did." I've got to forgive them. I still forgive them. My family and I still stand by what we believe: forgiveness.'[4]

In his Christmas sermon the Archbishop of Canterbury praised Mrs Walker's act of forgiveness. Dr Rowan Williams said, 'What made this so intensely moving was the fact that her forgiveness was drawn agonisingly out of her, without making her loss easier. She could not have been who she was if she did not recognise that forgiveness was laid upon her; her life and her dead son's would have been nonsense if she did not forgive. It was mercy without a hint of trivialisation or excuse for wrongdoing. No preacher could say it like that, could make it sound utterly true and costly and necessary all at once.'[5]

An ordained minister of the Gospel provides advice on the importance of forgiveness. He explains that many individuals are journeying through life with emotional and psychological stress and strain from a variety of past hurts. Some may have resentment or anger against a parent, relative, or friend who has 'wronged' them in the past. Holding on to negative feelings and attitudes has a direct effect on our health, whether we realise it or not. 'I suggest that you consider forgiveness as a powerful tool that can help. The ability, compassion and wisdom to forgive one another for past wrongs, hurts, and misunderstandings is one of the greatest attributes any of us can possess and exercise . . . When you and I truly and honestly forgive others for their wrongs toward us, we are set free in our own minds, souls, and spirits by our Creator in Heaven. You are really freeing yourself from the negative and unproductive feelings that hold you back from the blessings in store for you! The moment that one sincerely and freely forgives another, something wonderful and good happens to both the forgiver and the forgiven.'[6]

An article in *Evangelicals Now*, a Christian newspaper, describes the response of a father whose son was murdered in an incident at an asylum seeker's house in Manchester. 'When his father, a senior police officer and a Christian, was asked at a press conference what he thought of the man who had killed his son, he said calmly: "I forgive him." His reply caused astonishment among the journalists. *Christianity promises forgiveness to people and forgiveness is a hallmark of true Christianity.*'[7] (My italics.) The article goes on to claim that forgiveness is the unique characteristic of the Christian faith, for it is Christians alone who practise forgiveness.

There is no doubt that the examples quoted above represent a widespread notion that unconditional forgiveness is a central tenet of the Christian faith. Certainly Christians are commanded to love their enemies (in terms of pity and sympathy) and to pray for them, but not to declare absolution from sin, which is God's prerogative. To take this step may be well-intended, but it is mistaken.

In the secular world also there has been a growing interest in the supposed power of unconditional forgiveness, among psychologists, lawyers, politicians and moral philosophers. Therapeutic unconditional forgiveness is also widely promoted by positive psychology, New Age thinking and Eastern religions. Since the late 1990s the John Templeton Foundation has been awarding research grants for the study of forgiveness to a number of academic institutions.

What follows shows how this unbiblical idea of therapeutic forgiveness is being enthusiastically promoted by many organisations, as well as well-known evangelical writers.

Forgiveness research programme of the John Templeton Foundation

The John Templeton Foundation, which was established in 1987 from funds provided by the financial wizard and billionaire philanthropist Sir John, has in fact been the main driving force behind the worldwide rise in forgiveness research. The Foundation describes its mission as serving as a catalyst for discovery in areas engaging life's most important questions, with a special interest in the therapeutic benefits that flow from forgiveness.

In October 1997 the Foundation invited around 40 scholars to participate in a conference on the scientific study of forgiveness. Following the conference more than 100 research proposals were submitted and most received funding. Over the last 10 years the Foundation has supported the development of forgiveness protocols within the context of family relationships.

There is no question that funding from the wealthy Templeton Foundation has inspired a boom in forgiveness research. Before Templeton's interest in forgiveness, a search of the literature found only 50 studies even remotely related to the subject. At the last count, largely due to Templeton's money, there were nearly 4,500 studies relating to forgiveness.[8] Now there are numerous books on the subject, and there is even an International Forgiveness Institute. Clearly the resources and commitment of the John Templeton Foundation have played a pivotal role in stimulating the growing interest in forgiveness.

It is important to recognise that the underlying ethos of the Templeton Foundation is strongly New Age. The Foundation's Power of Purpose website explains that a growing number of people have an attachment to the concept of the divine spark. 'It is the sense that our lives can be guided from within by something more important than our simple survival, something not merely intellectual either, something in our souls.'[9] Sir John's New Age sentiments are clear from his comments on life and spirituality. He believes that the idea that an individual can find God is terribly self-centred. 'It is like a wave thinking it can find the sea.' Here is his view of God: 'The question is not, is there a God, but is there anything else except God? God is everyone and each of us is a little bit.' He asserted: 'The objective of our religious foundations is to teach people that they are hurting themselves when they say they believe something. What we should realise is we know almost nothing about God and therefore we should be eager to search and to learn.'[10]

Positive psychology

Positive psychology has also recently joined the forgiveness band-wagon. The positive psychology movement was born in 1998 when Martin Seligman became president of the American Psychological Association. His leadership helped to create a new and expanding branch of psychology that aims to shed light on the pursuit of happiness, and to show us how to lead more satisfying lives. Martin Seligman's landmark book, *Authentic Happiness* (2002), opens the way to this new branch of psychology that focuses on the good life, happiness and well-being.

In effect positive psychology is seeking the Holy Grail, the secret to a successful, happy life. It has a special interest in the power of forgiveness as a therapeutic tool that helps us feel good about ourselves.

A leading advocate of positive psychology is Dr Fred Luskin. As the Director of the Stanford Forgiveness Project, he developed a measurement scale for forgiveness interventions. Luskin's research has shown that forgiveness can reduce anger, hurt, depression and stress and lead to greater feelings of optimism, hope, compassion and self-confidence.[11] His book *Forgive For Good* (2002) describes 'Nine Steps to Forgiveness' the essential points of which are summarised below. Step one is to know exactly how you feel about what happened. Step two is to 'make a commitment to yourself to do what you have to do to feel better. Forgiveness is for you and not for anyone else. Forgiveness does not necessarily mean reconciliation with the person that upset you, or condoning of their action. What you are after is to find peace ... Recognise that your primary distress is coming from the hurt feelings, thoughts and physical upset you are suffering now, not what offended you or hurt you two minutes or ten years ago ...' The final steps are to look for another way to get your positive goals met other than through the experience that has hurt you. 'Instead of mentally replaying your hurt, seek out new ways to get what you want. Remember that a life well lived is your best revenge. Instead of focusing on your wounded feelings, and thereby giving the person who caused your pain power over you, learn to look for the love, beauty and kindness around you. Amend your grievance story to remind you of the heroic choice to forgive.'[12]

What Luskin has described is the therapeutic model of forgiveness, which is a new form of psychotherapy. The purpose of therapeutic forgiveness is to make you feel better. It revolves around you, helping you find peace of mind. It has nothing to do with reconciliation and is not concerned about the welfare of others. It is all about you achieving inner healing and getting what you want. As presented by Dr Luskin it is an entirely selfish enterprise.

The International Forgiveness Institute

Established in 1994 the International Forgiveness Institute has grown from the social research done at the University of Wisconsin-Madison by Robert Enright and his colleagues. The Institute, which receives generous research grants from the Templeton Foundation, serves as a forum for disseminating the findings of forgiveness research to as wide an audience as possible.

One output from the Institute is the *Enright Forgiveness Inventory Manual* which provides an objective measure of the degree to which one person forgives another who has hurt him deeply and unfairly. Another is the book *Helping Clients Forgive* (2000), which promotes forgiveness as a form of psychotherapy. Professor Enright comments that 'ten years ago it was rare for clients to come for therapy deliberately seeking help with forgiveness issues. More recently, this is changing as people read about or see on television stories of forgiveness and recon-ciliation. Yet the majority of clients still do not suggest forgiveness as an approach to anger reduction and healing. Therapists may have to take an active role here.'[13]

Professor Enright's *Forgiveness is a Choice* (2001), published by the American Psychological Association, is a self-help book for people who have been deeply hurt by another and caught in a vortex of anger, depression, and resentment. Enright proposes that forgiveness can reduce anxiety and depression while increasing self-esteem and hope-fulness toward one's future. He asserts that forgiveness, approached in the correct manner, benefits the forgiver far more than the forgiven.[14]

An article in the *Chicago Tribune*, based on the research work of the Forgiveness Institute, discussed the usefulness of forgiveness in emotional healing. The response was amazing. Within a week the Forgiveness Institute had hundreds of calls from people who had read the article and wanted information on how to forgive. *Time* magazine, *Christianity Today* and other media outlets ran major articles on forgiveness, highlighting the work of the Institute.

The Worldwide Forgiveness Alliance

The Worldwide Forgiveness Alliance, founded in 1996, is an educational foundation dedicated to evoking the healing power of forgiveness worldwide. An essential part of the Alliance's mission is to campaign for the establishment of the first global holiday, International Forgiveness Day, celebrated on the first Sunday of August.

The Alliance, open to all religions, creeds and beliefs, promotes forgiveness as a way of creating a safer, more joyful and peaceful world. It believes that it is time to establish an annual global holiday that signifies the transcendence of all division by encouraging the same universality and wholeness of spirit represented in the Whole Earth image. The Alliance advertises over 20 books on forgiveness, including *Total Forgiveness* (R. T. Kendall, discussed in the next chapter), *Radical Forgiveness* (Colin C. Tipping), *Forgive for Good* (Fred Luskin), *The Self-forgiveness Handbook* (Thom Rutledge), *Forgiveness: Breaking the Chain of Hate* (Michael Henderson) and *No Future without Forgiveness* (Desmond Tutu).

The Institute for Radical Forgiveness

The Institute for Radical Forgiveness Therapy and Coaching was founded by Colin and JoAnn Tipping in 1998. The purpose is to spread the message of radical forgiveness by training teachers, coaches and workshop leaders. According to Tipping we all need Radical Forgiveness. Why Radical Forgiveness? 'Because it works! It's as simple as that. If you're mad at someone, hurting, feeling victimised, depressed, grieving or angry, then Radical Forgiveness will give you the relief you are looking for . . . As you release the pain and self-destructive patterns that have kept you out of joy, stolen your life and blocked your abundance up to now, you will feel a profound feeling of inner peace and freedom.' And who should you forgive? 'Anyone you have an upset or grievance with, either in the past or right now, that you want resolved once and for all. Parents, partners, ex-partners, siblings, business partners, friends, doctors, lawyers, government officials, church leaders, the media, even God. And then, of course, there is always yourself.'[15]

Colin Tipping's book, *Radical Forgiveness* (1997), has become a bestseller, published in many languages. His mission is 'to raise the consciousness of the planet through Radical Forgiveness and to bring about a world of forgiveness by 2012'. He claims that Radical Forgiveness has really taken off and it is about to burst on to the world scene. 'I really believe that in the next few years we will reach the critical mass required for the breakthrough in consciousness that we all feel is imminent. Radical Forgiveness, I am convinced, will play a large part – along with many other spiritual technologies – so long as I can get enough people to spread the message and do the work.'[16]

The Forgiveness Project

The Forgiveness Project is a UK-based charitable organisation which explores forgiveness, reconciliation and conflict resolution through real-life human experience. The founder of the Project, journalist Marina Cantacuzino, acknowledges that without the generous funding of Anita Roddick (the Body Shop entrepreneur, proud of her New Age credentials)[17] the Forgiveness Project would not exist. When Roddick saw the stories of forgiveness she was so moved that she offered to fund the printing, production and launch of what became known as 'The F Word' exhibition that she described as 'truly an education of the human spirit'.[18] The exhibition, which was launched in London in 2004 to wide media acclaim, told the stories of people whose lives have been shattered by violence and tragedy who are learning to forgive. During two weeks, some 6,000 people visited the exhibition which received support from human rights activists, peace makers, religious figures and opinion formers.[19] The Project has collected over 60 personal stories of forgiveness since its launch and the exhibition has travelled widely and been staged at over 300 venues worldwide.

New Age forgiveness

Not many Christians understand that unconditional forgiveness is a central tenet of New Age thinking. The article 'True Forgiveness' describes the New Age approach. 'The spiritual purpose of forgiveness is self-healing. As long as we are holding anger, resentment and grudges against another person, we are poisoning our bodies with toxicity, lowering our immunity to disease and on subtler levels generating thoughts, expectations and attitudes that repel our highest good . . . Lack of forgiveness inhibits love, which is the only true source of power. As we withhold forgiveness, we inhibit our power and our very life-force.'[20]

The BellaOnline New Age website explains why unconditional forgiveness is important: 'Why should you forgive someone who has wronged you? Well there are several good reasons, other than the gazillion good karma points you earn!

'First and foremost you need to *forgive because it is good for you.* While you are still angry and resentful of a person you are energetically connected with them. At a subtle energy level they have got their hooks into you. Letting go of the anger and sending forgiveness instead releases the energy connection and frees you of the energetic drain.

'Holding on to resentment and anger can literally make you ill too. It can weigh you down. If you can let go of it you will instantly feel lighter and freer. Sometimes a person can have been so abusive towards you that your very human ego self can't find forgiveness for them. If this is the case then ask for your Higher Self, your spiritual self, to send the forgiveness. From a higher perspective this can always be done. *Forgiveness is a gift to yourself.*'[21] (My italics.)

Eastern religions

In the Hindu religion forgiveness is the highest virtue. According to the *Mahabharata*, 'the man of wisdom should ever forgive, for when he is capable of forgiving everything, he attains to Brahma. The world belongs to those that are forgiving; the other world is also theirs . . . The forgiving acquire honours here, and a state of blessedness hereafter. Those men that ever conquer their wrath by forgiveness obtain the higher regions. Therefore has it been said that forgiveness is the highest virtue.'[22]

A key aspect of Transcendental Meditation is the practice of unconditional forgiveness. 'It's important to forgive unconditionally. Saying you forgive a person if she changes her behaviour is conditional forgiveness.

This creates a hidden slow poison that later manifests in the relationship as a dangerous, deadly sickness.'

'The heart craves unconditional forgiveness. The mind is always trying to set some conditions, but if you forgive someone unconditionally it will be more healing for yourself. If you practise this over time, your overall attitude and behaviour will become more nourishing – and that helps build and maintain relationships. Unconditional forgiveness keeps the mind under the influence of the heart. That's what you need in relationships – your heart predominating over your mind.'[23]

Forgiveness for all

In this chapter we have gone to some length to demonstrate the worldwide campaign to promote unconditional forgiveness. Clearly the assertion by *Evangelicals Now* that forgiveness is a uniquely Christian characteristic is not true. While the forgiveness of sin has always been uniquely Christian, the last two decades have seen a massive increase in the idea of therapeutic forgiveness. This renewed interest has been driven to a large degree by positive psychology and New Age thinking, with generous funding from the vast resources of the John Templeton Foundation. The question is to what degree the new-found belief in unconditional forgiveness among Christians has come from New Age thinking.

7

A Biblical Critique of Therapeutic Forgiveness

WE HAVE SEEN in the previous chapter that there is a popular view among Christians that our faith requires that we forgive anyone who offends us. Yet the idea that Christians are required to practise unconditional forgiveness is a relatively new phenomenon. In his book *Total Forgiveness* (2002), considered below, R. T. Kendall points out that as a minister of the Gospel he had read hundreds of sermons by the Puritans and the Reformers, yet he cannot recall being told by them that he must totally forgive or otherwise grieve the Holy Spirit. Even his godly parents did not teach him the wonders of total forgiveness. 'Not a single mentor (that I can recall) emphasised this as a lifestyle.'[1]

Here then is the dilemma. Did the church in past centuries overlook the duty of total forgiveness? Or, is it possible that Christians who follow the newly-discovered doctrine of total forgiveness are being influenced by New Age thinking? In this chapter we examine the Christian response to the forgiveness bandwagon.

A plethora of books and articles exhort Christians to follow the pathway of total forgiveness. Lewis Smedes, professor emeritus of theology and ethics at Fuller Seminary, was one of the first to write on the subject. His book *Forgive and Forget: Healing the Hurts We Don't Deserve* (1984) shows that it is possible to heal our pain and find room in our hearts to forgive.[2] *The Art of Forgiving: When You Need to Forgive and Don't Know How* (1996), also by Lewis Smedes, is written from a Christian perspective, but is furnished with modern therapeutic insights. 'Using many dramatic examples drawn from life, this wise author illuminates, step by step, the healing path to peace.'[3]

Christian psychiatrist Frank Minirth and Les Carter have produced *The Choosing to Forgive Workbook* (1997) which uses methods 'to help you truly forgive those who've wronged you. The workbook will teach you how to increase your ability to forgive . . . This new 12-step plan will guide you through elements that are crucial to forgiveness and healing . . . choose forgiveness and start on the path toward a life of abundance.'[4]

The New Freedom of Forgiveness (2000) by David Augsburger, commands us to forgive everything, not just the little stuff, the minor irritations and thoughtless behaviour of others, but everything. When we forgive, it insists, we are set free from bondage. This 'life-changing' book is promoted as an essential resource for understanding what God requires. *Choosing Forgiveness* (2006) by Nancy Leigh DeMoss presents powerful, real-life stories to help readers understand the fullness of God's mercy and forgiveness in their own hearts. The author explains that for us to forgive like God is a choice that frees us from the burdens of bitterness, anger, and isolation.

The charismatic movement is deeply committed to the promotion of forgiveness and inner healing. The pastor of the Toronto Airport Church, John Arnot, has written *The Importance of Forgiveness* (1997) and *Forgiveness: Biblical Truth Explained* (2003). He teaches that Christians need inner healing and forgiveness. He believes that anger or estrangement toward parents or family members, who have hurt us in the past, sometimes repeatedly over the years, is a cause of hidden unforgiveness which inevitably stands in the way of a believer's full surrender to God's inner or physical healing.[5]

A seminal book is R. T. Kendall's *Total Forgiveness* (2002), already mentioned. R. T. Kendall was the Pastor of the famous Westminster

Chapel in Central London for 25 years, which during his ministry turned into a fully charismatic church.

'Total Forgiveness'

Total Forgiveness is important because it represents the view of forgiveness that is now widely held by huge numbers of Christians. Kendall believes that it is the most important book he has written, being 'by far the book that has the greatest potential to heal the human heart'.[6]

A *Daily Express* headline, 'Can you learn to forgive?' (5th June 2000), had a large impact on the thinking of Kendall. A lecturer at Leeds University, Dr Ken Hart, had been running the world's first forgiveness course, designed to help people forgive their enemies and let go of grudges.[7] In Kendall's mind this was an example of non-believers doing something biblical without knowing it. 'There are indications that the world is starting to recognise the merit of forgiving people and it may be that it is Christians who are lagging behind. Sadly, for too long this included me.'[8] Here we should note that the forgiveness research of Dr Hart, which so impressed Kendall, was funded by the Templeton Foundation.

Kendall openly confesses that he had bitterness in his heart against people whom he felt had wronged him. 'The wrong that I believe was done to me hit just about every area of my life: my family, my ministry, my very sense of self-worth.'[9] His Romanian friend, Pastor Josef Tson, advised, 'RT you must totally forgive them. Until you totally forgive them you will be in chains. Release them and you will be set free.'[10] Kendall explains that he had to make an important decision. 'Which do I prefer – the peace or the bitterness? I couldn't have it both ways. I began to see that I was the great loser – the impoverished one – by not forgiving. My bitterness wasn't damaging anyone but myself.'[11] Kendall continues, 'I made a decision for inner peace, but I found that I had to carry that decision by a daily commitment to forgive those who had hurt me, and to forgive them totally. I therefore let them utterly off the hook and resigned myself to the knowledge that, first, they wouldn't get caught or found out; second, nobody would ever know what they did; and, third, they would prosper and be blessed as though they had done no wrong. What is more, I actually willed this! I prayed for this! I asked

God to forgive them. But I had to do it every day in order to keep the peace within my heart.'[12]

Kendall has a classic view of therapeutic forgiveness. The reason he granted forgiveness was in order to achieve inner peace for himself, and those he forgave were unaware of the forgiveness he had silently granted in his heart. So those who were supposed to have caused the offence were untouched by his forgiveness. Reform and reconciliation was not part of R. T. Kendall's new view of total forgiveness.

Kendall believes that the ultimate proof of total forgiveness 'is when we sincerely petition the Father to let off the hook those who have hurt us – even if they have hurt those close to us'.[13] He explains that total forgiveness is painful. 'But when I know fully what they did, and accept in my heart that they will be blessed without any consequences for their wrong, I have crossed over into the supernatural. This means I have begun to be a little like Jesus.'[14] An essential aspect of total forgiveness is refusing to punish. 'Total forgiveness is graciousness that will sometimes mean overlooking the truth and not letting on that you know anything that could damage a person in any way.'[15]

Kendall teaches that a Christian can ask God to forgive (let off the hook) someone who has not repented and confessed their sin. It seems that he wants God to bless unrepentant wrongdoers. He even wants Christians to deny the truth in order to avoid any possibility that a wrongdoer will be punished for his sin.

Total forgiveness must take place in the heart. Moreover, reconciliation is not always essential. 'If it takes place in the heart, one does not need to know whether one's enemy will reconcile. If I have forgiven him or her in my heart of hearts, and he doesn't want to speak to me, I can still have the inner victory.'[16] Kendall's own experience is that 'most people we must forgive do not believe they have done anything wrong whatsoever; or if they did something wrong they believe it was justifiable. I would go so far as to say that 90 per cent (at least) of all the people I've ever had to forgive would be indignant at the thought that they had done something wrong . . . if those who hurt me don't want to make up, that isn't my problem when I have totally forgiven them. This is why a person can achieve victory (within) even in the case of forgiving the person who has died.'[17]

Here Christians are exhorted to silently forgive those who they feel have offended them, without any attempt at reconciliation. Moreover, how easy it is for us to create imaginary offences in order to make us feel good when we graciously forgive the non-existent offence. Notice that the practice of total forgiveness appears to be totally unconcerned that Christians are unable to be reconciled. As long as the forgiving person feels better, that is all that matters.

Total forgiveness, in Kendall's thinking, also involves forgiving God. He says, 'The truth is, our bitterness is often aimed at God. Why? Because he allowed bad things to happen . . . He has allowed us to suffer when we didn't do anything that we know of to warrant such ill-treatment. Therefore what we are ultimately thinking is that God is to blame for our hurt . . . We therefore must forgive him – but not because he is guilty, but for allowing evil to touch our lives.'[18] The idea that a human being can have the effrontery to forgive God beggars the imagination. The very thought produces a proud arrogant spirit in man, who sees himself in a position to forgive the Almighty. 'Shall the one who contends with the Almighty correct Him? He who rebukes God, let him answer it' *(Job 40.2)*.

Even then total forgiveness is not complete, for we still need to forgive ourselves. Kendall explains, 'But I must say here and now: there is no lasting joy in forgiveness if it doesn't include forgiving myself. It is anything but total forgiveness if we forgive God and those who have hurt us, but are unable to forgive ourselves. It is as wrong as not forgiving others, because God loves us as much as he does others and will be as unhappy when we don't forgive ourselves as when we hold a grudge against others.'[19] The disturbing feature of this teaching is that it presses and encourages Christians to focus on self.

Kendall sums up his doctrine of forgiveness. 'Total forgiveness brings such joy and satisfaction that one is tempted to call it a selfish enterprise. As we have seen, the wider research that is taking place these days has already overwhelmingly concluded that the first person to experience delight when forgiveness takes place is the one who forgives.'[20] Kendall's dogma of forgiveness is indeed a selfish enterprise. Total forgiveness is psychological therapy to make us feel good – it is pure New Age thinking in Christian clothes that understands nothing about the nature of sin and the cost of true forgiveness through the Cross of Christ.

Concerning R. T. Kendall and others who write as he does, one is bound to ask why they go well into their adult life nurturing bitter thoughts about all the people who have hurt them in some way. Is it our own pride or self-pity that hangs on to a multitude of resentments? Surely it is not a matter of extending sentimental forgiveness to the alleged offender, but of being less touchy, less sensitive, less inclined to nurse wounds and grievances, less ready to hold others accountable for our difficulties. The answer is not secret forgiveness, but more gratitude to God for his overwhelming kindness and favour to us, and prayer for greater resilience, and greater concern for the troubles of other people, as well as for the great priorities of spiritual usefulness in God's service.

The Christian counselling movement

It should come as no surprise that the Christian counselling movement has latched on to the agenda of therapeutic forgiveness. According to James Dobson, 'Psychologists and ministers now agree that there is only one cure for the cancer of bitterness. It is to forgive, which Dr Archibald Hart defines as "giving up my right to hurt you for hurting me". Only when we find the emotional maturity to release those who have wronged us, whether they have repented or not, will the wounds finally start to heal.'[21]

Christian psychiatrists Frank Minirth and Paul Meier in *Happiness is a Choice* (1994) explain that *Matthew 5.21-24* teaches that '*we must forgive no matter what response* we get from the other person. Why should we suffer depression for *his sin*? That would be foolish. We should verbalise our anger and forgive him whether he deserves forgiveness or not. This will keep us from becoming depressed.'[22] (Their italics.) According to Minirth and Meier the purpose of unconditional forgiveness is that we benefit. Why should we suffer because of our brother?

Dr Stanley M. Giannet, who holds a doctorate in clinical psychology and a Master's of Ministry in Christian Counselling, says, 'forgiveness is an essential feature of psychological health. A well-adjusted and pious person practises forgiveness whenever confronted with interpersonal conflict. This is an important value not only because of universal ethics and Christian ideals, but also because the suppression of anger can emotionally cripple an individual indelibly.'[23]

In his book *Healing of Memories*, David Seamands relates the story of a young couple who came for counselling. The problem was that they kept hurting each other. Seamands soon realised that the wife, Mitzi, 'was one deep reservoir of pain waiting to be tapped into. All her life, pastors and teachers had told her to just forget the past, claim victory in Christ, and develop new skills for coping with the present and future.' But Seamands tapped into her repressed memories that he felt were causing her pain. 'One by one, Mitzi visualised before the Lord some of her most hurtful and humiliating childhood and teenage experiences . . . She was re-living and re-feeling incidents, often in remarkable detail, *as if she were actually there now*. Although it was a struggle, Mitzi was forgiving the many people who had hurt her; and in turn, she was receiving God's forgiveness for her long-held resentments against them.'[24] This experience, according to Seamands, was the turning point in her life. Seamands claims that when specific memories have been allowed to surface, resulting in specific confession of specific feelings and specific forgiveness, the result is deep inner healing and cleansing.[25]

According to Seamands the Christian counsellor must help his clients to forgive themselves. 'Sometimes the greatest battle is not in forgiving those who have hurt us, or in receiving God's forgiveness for our hates, but in trying to forgive ourselves . . . Here again, counsellors must emphasise the will to forgive ourselves, and the commitment to continue doing this.'[26]

At the centre of the Christian counselling movement is a commitment to a therapeutic view of forgiveness. Total forgiveness is seen as a psychotherapeutic intervention that helps us feel better, that gives us inner peace, that sets us free. It is not difficult to see that there is little difference in the New Age version of total forgiveness and that of the Christian counselling movement.

What the Bible teaches about forgiveness

We have seen that unconditional forgiveness is not a defining characteristic of the Christian faith. Our task now is to examine what the Bible teaches about forgiveness. But here we need to understand that there is great confusion in the church around the issue of forgiveness, and many Bible teachers have been influenced by psychologisers and liberal theologians. We should also recognise that there is a link between unconditional love and unconditional forgiveness. Those who teach the one are also likely to preach the other. Yet in a search of classic works on systematic theology we are unlikely to find any mention of unconditional forgiveness for it is a new concept that has been promoted only in recent decades.

As Scripture has perspicuity it is possible for God's people to understand the biblical view of forgiveness. To help our thinking we first need to understand God's forgiveness of human sin, for only then can we understand Christian forgiveness of those who offend against us.

Forgiveness in the Garden of Eden

To return to the Garden of Eden, we see no sign of unconditional forgiveness on God's part. According to Scripture, God alone has the power to forgive sin. God, therefore, could have immediately forgiven Adam unconditionally if he so decided. But he did not do so. Why? A God who practised unconditional forgiveness could have said, 'Because I'm a loving, gracious God, Adam, you are unconditionally forgiven. Forgive me for setting you such a difficult moral test of obedience. From now on you are free to eat of any tree you choose.' In other words, God could have accepted and tolerated Adam's sin. It is obvious, however, that if God had forgiven Adam's sin unconditionally, he would have shown himself to be an amoral God who condones sin, and that is not the character of the God of the Bible.

But God, who is rich in mercy, in the Garden of Eden revealed his gracious plan of salvation from sin – a Saviour, the Seed of the woman, whose heel would be bruised on the cross, would bruise the head of Satan *(Genesis 3.15)*. God has provided a way to pay the price demanded for sin, through the Seed of the woman. Jesus Christ became sin for us when he died on the cross; he died in our place. God's justice was satisfied and the penalty of sin paid. God's forgiveness is only through the Cross of Christ. We have redemption through the blood of Christ, and the forgiveness of sin. Without the shedding of blood there is no forgiveness. God now commands all men everywhere to repent and turn to Christ to obtain forgiveness of their sins. So God's forgiveness is conditional on the Cross of Christ. Other than by the Cross, there is no forgiveness.

Oswald Chambers warns of the danger of a view of forgiveness based on a false view of God. 'Beware of the pleasant view of the fatherhood of God: God is so kind and loving that of course he will forgive us. That thought, based solely on emotion, cannot be found anywhere in the New Testament . . . Forgiveness is the divine miracle of grace. The cost to God was the Cross of Christ. To forgive sin, while remaining a holy God, this price had to be paid. Never accept a view of the fatherhood of God if it blots out the atonement. The revealed truth of God is that without the atonement he cannot forgive – he would contradict his nature if he did.'[27]

An essential feature of God's forgiveness is that we are reconciled with God and enter into a relationship with God as his adopted children. 'God was in Christ reconciling the world to Himself, not imputing their trespasses to them, and has committed to us the word of reconciliation' *(2 Corinthians 5.19)*. Forgiveness and reconciliation always go together. Indeed, the purpose of forgiveness is to restore the relationship that has been broken by sin. Only God's redeemed people know the wonder of forgiveness from sin. While God's forgiveness is undeserved, it certainly is not unconditional, for the Lord's forgiveness is offered only to those who confess their sin and truly repent. 'If My people who are called by My name will humble themselves, and pray and seek My face, and *turn from their wicked ways*, then I will hear from heaven, and will forgive their sin and heal their land' *(2 Chronicles 7.14)*. The condition is clear: 'If My people repent, then I will forgive their sin.' God's forgiveness is conditional upon repentance. Scripture makes it clear – if we confess our sins, God is faithful and just to forgive us our sins and to cleanse us from all unrighteousness *(1 John 1.8-10)*. This is God's Truth. This is God's way to forgiveness and there is no other.

A forgiving attitude

As forgiven sinners, all Christians have an understanding of what it is to receive God's gracious unmerited forgiveness. We also know what it has cost God our Father to forgive us. For this reason Christians, as those who have been forgiven much, in their gratitude to God, know that they should have the same attitude to others. As God has forgiven us much so we should be willing to forgive those who sin against us. Christians are to have a gracious, forgiving heart, like their Lord. This is the great biblical principle.

The Bible tells us that we should forgive as the Lord forgave us *(Colossians 3.13)*. As we have already seen, the Lord's forgiveness is offered only to those who regret their sin and truly repent.

An essential aspect of forgiveness is that it restores a relationship. When a Christian offends against a brother in Christ the relationship is affected. We have the example of the apostle Peter who denied his Lord. He knew that he had done wrong, and this is why he wept bitterly. When Jesus approached him on the seashore it was with the purpose of forgiving a deeply repentant Peter and restoring the relationship.

Forgiving our brother

The Bible teaches that Christians are one in Christ. The essential characteristic of believers is that we love one another. As Christ laid down his life for us, we ought to lay down our lives for the brethren *(1 John 3.16)*. When a Christian sins against a brother the Bible provides clear instructions. 'Take heed to yourselves. If your brother sins against you, rebuke him; and if he repents, forgive him. And if he sins against you seven times in a day, and seven times in a day returns to you, saying, "I repent", you shall forgive him' *(Luke 17.3-4)*. Notice the command of Christ – if your brother sins against you, rebuke him. Why? To make it absolutely clear that the sin is not tolerated, but also to allow for forgiveness and reconciliation. Christ's specific teaching about forgiveness makes it clear that forgiveness should follow repentance – if your brother repents, then forgive him. The Lord deals with the situation where there is no repentance. 'Moreover if your brother sins against you, go and tell him his fault between you and him alone. If he hears you, you have gained your brother. But if he will not hear, take with you one or two more, that "by the mouth of two or three witnesses every word may be established". And if he refuses to hear them, tell it to the church. But if he refuses even to hear the church, let him be to you like a heathen and a tax collector' *(Matthew 18.15-17)*.

Clearly, where there is no repentance there can be no forgiveness. Indeed, the unrepentant brother is to be treated like a tax collector. Scripture forbids the unconditional forgiveness of an unrepentant offending brother. We must bear in mind that this passage of Scripture is talking about *sinful* conduct, and conduct so serious as to warrant excommunication if not repented of. It is not talking about lesser offences that are better absorbed and forgotten under the principle that love covers the multitude of sins.

So there is no silent forgiveness of a Christian who has seriously and deliberately sinned against another. The offence is faced and dealt with in order to achieve reconciliation. The brother who has been sinned against goes to his brother in a spirit of love, ready to forgive. The idea that a Christian ignores this biblical teaching and silently declares his brother forgiven, as R. T. Kendall advises, is contrary to Scripture. It is New Age forgiveness that has no place in the church of Jesus Christ.

The Christian and the unbeliever

The relationship between Christians and unbelievers is completely different. Christians are the forgiven, redeemed children of God, indwelt by the Holy Spirit; the unbeliever is spiritually dead and a slave of sin. The world of unbelief will revile and persecute Christians and falsely say all kinds of evil against them *(Matthew 5.11)*, but Christ taught his followers that they must love their enemies. 'But I say to you . . . bless those who curse you, do good to those who hate you, and pray for those who spitefully use you and persecute you, that you may be sons of your Father in heaven; for He makes His sun rise on the evil and on the good, and sends rain on the just and on the unjust' *(Matthew 5.44-45)*.

The responsibility of the Christian is to love his enemies, and to pray for them, that God will open their eyes to see their need to obtain forgiveness of sin through the Cross of Christ. Nowhere in Scripture is the Christian told to unconditionally forgive an unbeliever who sins against him. To do so is only a meaningless gesture; for by what authority does a Christian forgive sin? This only leads to a false view of forgiveness, and the world will gain the idea that Christians practise cheap forgiveness, like New Age adherents. For Christians to offer unconditional forgiveness to all and sundry is to make a mockery of the Cross of Christ.

At the start of the previous chapter we saw examples of gesture forgiveness. While it is too often wrongly believed that unconditional forgiveness is the hallmark of Christian conduct, nothing could be further from the truth. Such is the pressure of the unconditional forgiveness lobby that Christians feel obliged to publicly declare their forgiveness for the most wicked of crimes, and even to forgive people who continue in their sin. Christians now feel obliged to forgive all who sin against them, no matter what. Christians are even expected to forgive those whom God has not forgiven. But is this right? Of course not!

The moral wrongness of unconditional forgiveness is that it condones sin and wrongdoing. The wrongdoer is not held accountable for his sin, but actually encouraged to believe that it is a light matter. The sad truth is that the toleration of sin implicit in unconditional forgiveness can be destructive. If a wife continues to forgive a habitually unfaithful and abusive husband unconditionally, her toleration of his behaviour will probably result in even more abuse and disrespect. Her passive acceptance of his behaviour may well encourage him to continue in his sin. Instead of her forgiveness being helpful, it actually tolerates sin and stands in the way of repentance and reconciliation.

Christians should be careful not to follow the way of the world. We should not be deceived by the forgiveness bandwagon promoted by New Age thinking. We should stick close to the teaching of the Bible and follow the example of the apostle Paul, who tells us that Alexander the coppersmith did him much harm. Did Paul forgive him unconditionally? On the contrary, Paul prayed that God would repay Alexander according to his works. There was no unconditional forgiveness from the great apostle, who wrote that we should forgive as the Lord forgave us.

Christians should not publicly declare that they forgive sins where there is no repentance on the part of the offender. Such unconditional forgiveness is an offence against justice and a denial of the significance of sin and its cruel effects. Indeed, it is not true forgiveness but gesture forgiveness. And gesture forgiveness, though sometimes well-intended, is really the tolerance of wrong. In a flawed world, forgiveness should never be given unconditionally. Having said that, Christians should always be willing to share the gracious forgiveness they have received through Christ. We should seek to love those who hate us and despitefully use us, pray for them, and respond to them in a way that is ultimately in their best interest.

Counterfeit New Age forgiveness

Scripture is clear that only God can forgive sin, and without the blood of Christ there is no forgiveness. New Age forgiveness stands in direct opposition to Scripture's view of forgiveness, for it propagates the idea that we all have the power to forgive ourselves, others and even God. The purpose behind New Age forgiveness is to diminish the seriousness of sin, to suggest forgiveness without repentance. But this is counterfeit forgiveness. It is an entirely selfish enterprise that detracts from the Gospel. Christians should not only have nothing to do with counterfeit, unconditional forgiveness, they should expose it for the fraud that it is.

8
Theories of the Marriage Education Movement

WE NOW TURN to the marriage education movement that is an important arm of the psychotherapeutic mission in both the USA and the UK and other Western nations. Indeed, marriage and family therapy has become the second most common psychotherapeutic enterprise after cognitive behavioural therapy (see chapter 10). The number of people attending marriage education courses far outnumbers those seeking help for depression. It is no surprise, then, that marriage and family issues have become a major sector for the psychotherapeutic world.

Marriage and family therapy

The early work of the American Association of Marriage and Family Therapy (AAMFT) revolved around providing psychotherapy for people involved in unhappy marriages. Psychotherapists were accepted as experts who were able to offer advice to those who were thinking of divorce. The message was that a good divorce is better than a bad marriage. The idea of trying to save a crumbling marriage was regarded as an archaic belief that had no place in the modern world. An article in

the *New York Times* in 1967 said it all: 'Marriage counsellors and psychotherapists have been adopting the view that where a marriage seems
unlikely ever to become satisfying and reasonably free of conflicts, it is
proper to help the client get out of it.' The article went on to describe
divorce counsellors as the surgeons of marriage, wielding the knife
when necessary. Those who believed that they should stay together for
the sake of the children were considered mistaken because the evidence
gathered by marriage experts pointed in exactly the opposite direction.[1]
The mantra, 'divorce for the sake of the children', although based on
flawed psychological research, led to a massive increase in the divorce
rate in the 1970s and 1980s.

But divorce counselling did not lead to the promised land of psychological healing. On the contrary, the misery caused by widespread
divorce, obvious to all, forced the psychotherapeutic world to rethink
its approach. Something had to be done, because marriage and divorce
counselling was rapidly losing credibility. It was at this time that a
perceptive journalist asked a Director of the Association, named Diane
Sollee, why, with so many marriage therapists being trained and registered, the divorce rate was not going down. Sollee was unable to answer
the question, for she knew that when it came to helping couples find
ways of staying together, marriage and family therapists were highly
ineffective. She realised that her profession was in trouble. An article in
the *Psychotherapeutic Networker* comments: 'What pulled her out of the
crisis over her professional direction was learning about a new wave of
educational and skills-training programmes that took direct aim at the
high divorce rate by teaching couples strategies for dealing with marital
conflict before they landed in a therapist's office or in divorce court.
Soon Sollee was a convert, and even gave the new movement a name:
marriage education.'[2]

Marriage education

After ten years as a family therapist at the AAMFT, Diane Sollee,
herself a divorcee, decided to propagate her new-found faith in
marriage education. Her ambition was to expand the visibility of these
programmes around the USA, so in 1996 she founded the Coalition
for Marriage, Family and Couples Education, with the aim of making
marriage education a household word.

At the same time, a great change in social attitude spurred on the new style of marriage education. During the last decades of the twentieth century the institution of marriage came under a sustained attack in both Britain and the USA from feminists, secular humanists and psychotherapists who were ideologically opposed to marriage. Traditional marriage was portrayed as the foundation of the patriarchal society. Feminist commentators, such as Germaine Greer and Betty Friedan, claimed that marriage is a cause of women's oppression. They argued that marriage is based on sexual inequality, and therefore a form of bondage that inhibits a wife's ability to express herself as a person.

Yet the serious social problems caused by mass divorce, the failure of marital therapy to increase the sum of human happiness, and a realisation that most people still wanted to get married, led to a re-evaluation of the ideological opposition to marriage. Secular opponents came to realise that what they really objected to was the biblical view of marriage that gives different roles to husband and wife. The concept of the husband as the head of the family, and the wife who willingly submits to his headship, was anathema to the secular, feminist mindset and had to be brought to an end. So those who opposed traditional marriage became content to accept a secular version of 'marriage' based on sexual equality. And so the marriage education movement established its ideological ground – secular, equal-regard marriage is a useful relationship model, while biblical, oppressive marriage is beyond the pale. Based on this ideological position, a wide variety of marriage education programmes are now available in the USA and the UK.

The human potential movement and marriage enrichment

Marriage enrichment, the forerunner of marriage education, was first developed in the USA in the 1970s as an off-shoot of the humanistic psychology of Rogers and Maslow. These two giants of psychotherapy taught that human nature was basically good with an innate potential for positive growth. Their anti-biblical thinking provided the philosophical foundation for the human potential movement, of which marriage enrichment has become an important arm.[3]

Richard Hunt, the Professor of Psychology at Fuller Seminary, acknowledges the role of humanistic psychology and the human potential movement in forming a foundation for the marriage enrichment process. He also accepts the link between Rogerian psychotherapy and marriage enrichment programmes where 'participants can freely express their feelings and experience increased self-acceptance and knowledge, and increased acceptance of others and from others, especially their marital partner.'[4]

Marriage enrichment, faithful to the human potential movement, holds an optimistic view of human nature that sees positive change as possible. 'People are viewed as having a natural drive toward growth, health, and personal development.'[5] The goal of marriage enrichment is to help couples develop techniques that achieve self-growth and happiness. We are called upon to reject all negative thoughts that place a limit on human potential. Our minds are to be reprogrammed by daily affirmations, by positive optimistic thinking, and by constant self-talk. We must persuade ourselves that we have the innate ability to achieve truly happy relationships. We can have great marriages if we learn a set of psychological skills and set our minds to it.

At the heart of marriage enrichment are communication skills that mean 'effective, deep sharing of feelings, thoughts, wants, needs, and intentions between partners'.[6] The aim is to teach partners how to communicate fully on intellectual and emotional levels. Most programmes teach conflict resolution skills and believe that responsible confrontation can have beneficial results. Couples are taught 'how to rechannel conflict and confrontation into a positive experience, albeit one that is frequently painful'.[7]

Here we see the two fundamental flaws of the marriage enrichment movement. The first is the false premise that humans have the innate potential to experience a quality of life filled with happiness, creativity and inner peace. Theoretically, society can reform itself. This premise denies the doctrine of original sin and does not recognise that underlying all conflict are the sins and lusts of the flesh that lie deep in the human heart (Galatians 5.19-21).

The second false premise is the idea of self-improvement – the idea that sinful men and women can improve themselves and their relationships without the spiritual transformation that is brought about by a new life in Christ. But the Bible teaches that those who are dead in sin cannot greatly improve themselves, for they are slaves to sin, and incapable of really breaking the power of sin that rules in their lives. It is faith in Christ alone that breaks the power of sin.

Coalition for Marriage, Family and Couples Education

As mentioned above, the Coalition for Marriage, Family and Couples Education was founded in 1996 by Diane Sollee, an eminent marriage and family therapist. The Coalition is a secular organisation that hosts the annual 'Smart Marriages, Happy Families' conference. The website of the Coalition, which provides information on around 60 teach-out-of-the-box programmes, claims to be the ultimate resource guide for finding premarital and marriage enrichment programmes. It also provides information for cohabiting couples to help them develop the skills they need to have a more stable and long-lasting relationship.[8]

According to Sollee, the long-term aim of the Coalition is to change 'the way the culture thinks about marriage'. The unspoken agenda is for the old hierarchical (biblical) view of marriage to be replaced with a more equitable relationship. The marriage education movement aims to get the message into every part of society.

In an interview Sollee explained that the Coalition drives a secular agenda that regards all types of relationships – that is married, cohabiting and same-sex relationships – as moral equivalents. 'In fact, at the conference I make sure every year there is a gay-lesbian presentation about how these same skills work in those relationships.'[9] Although religious and non-religious people attend the conference, they all leave their belief system or ideology at the door. Needless to say, the Coalition does not support the biblical view of marriage.

Couple Relationship Education in the UK

In the UK the annual National Relationship Education Conference, held since 2002, brings together a number of organisations that share an interest in what is called 'couple relationship education', and this is effectively the British arm of what we have just described in the USA. Participants in the conference have included Relate, the largest provider of relationship support services in the UK, One Plus One, that advises government on relationship issues and family, and also parenting support organisations such as Parenting UK, Positive Parenting, Care for the Family, Marriage Care, and Alpha. The conference is attended by both Christian and secular organisations.

The report, 'Building Strong Foundations – The Case for Couple Relationship Education' (2009) was written to make a case for a much greater commitment to the provision of relationship education across the UK.[10] It claims that – 'A successful intimate long-term relationship . . . requires basic skills which it can no longer be assumed that people acquire from family and friends. Many will require specific training if they are to have the opportunity of a stable committed relationship.'[11]

The increasing reluctance of the UK government to support traditional marriage means that couple relationship education does not emphasise marriage above any other type of relationship.[12] Nevertheless the report does point out that the Marriage Course (discussed in the next chapter) 'is the most widely used single programme, with over 1,000 course providers identified as having been trained and/or offering their course in the UK.'[13]

It is important to understand that the couple relationship education movement in the UK is made up of both secular organisations, such as Relate and Parenting UK, along with Christian organisations, such as Care for the Family and the Marriage Course. This togetherness is only possible because the Christian organisations engaged in couple relationship education do not take a stand for the truly biblical view of marriage.

Theological seminaries and family therapy

Many theological seminaries in the USA have courses on marriage and family therapy, largely taken from secular psychology, and have become an important part of the marriage education movement. The large number of therapists and counsellors trained in these settings are taking the ideology of marriage education into churches across the USA.

These seminaries graduate thousands upon thousands of people who are indoctrinated in the teachings of the marriage education movement. Indeed, the training provided by American Christian theological colleges is so in line with the secular world that most graduates meet all the educational requirements of the American Association for Marriage and Family Therapy.

Today marriage education has become a massive industry in the USA with literally hundreds of organisations providing psychologically orientated education models claiming to improve marriage and cohabiting relationships. A few selected examples will illustrate the features of the marriage education movement.

The PREP

The Prevention and Relationship Enhancement Programme (PREP), described in *Fighting for your Marriage* (2001), by Professor Howard Markman and other psychologists, aims to help couples build happy and strong marriages. The authors assert, 'We are known for taking solid research findings and translating them into usable, specific, and powerful strategies to help couples preserve a lasting love. If you are in a relationship, our goal is to help you with practical, no-nonsense advice. If you are someone who works with couples (such as a counsellor or clergy member), our goal is to give you clear and consistent strategies for having a powerful impact with couples.'[14] The aim is to teach 'how to walk the deeper paths of commitment, forgiveness and friendship. When you walk these paths together, you will find happiness and love throughout your journey.'[15]

Christian PREP claims to reflect 'a clear commitment to traditional Christianity and Christian truth'. However, Christian PREP avoids the role of husband (headship) and wife (submission) taught in Scripture *(Ephesians 5.22-33, Colossians 3.18-19* and *1 Peter 3.1-7)*. The reason that PREP does not teach the biblical view of marriage is because to do so would reveal the enormous gulf between Scripture and the marriage education movement.

Imago Relationship Therapy

Imago Therapy was developed in the 1980s by psychotherapist Dr Harville Hendrix in the USA and has spread worldwide. His bestselling book *Getting The Love You Want* (1988) describes the Imago system as one that invites every couple to realise that the purpose of their relationship is to help one another. Hendrix's system brings 'together depth psychology, the behavioural sciences, the Western spiritual tradition, and added some elements of Transactional Analysis, Gestalt psychology, systems theory and cognitive therapy'.[16]

Imago therapy is a mishmash of psychological theories with a strong Freudian emphasis on the so-called unconscious marriage. The ideas of inner healing and human growth come from the humanistic psychology of Rogers and Maslow. This misguided programme is feeding couples with psychological theories that reflect no understanding of the true nature of marriage.

The PREPARE/ENRICH programme

The PREPARE programme is the brainchild of Dr David Olson, a licensed psychologist and Fellow of the American Psychological Association, with over 30 years' experience in the field of marriage and family therapy. Dr Olson developed the psychological questionnaire PREPARE for premarital couples in 1977, and later the ENRICH questionnaire for married couples. The PREPARE/ENRICH programme provides a range of tools for counsellors, clergy members, mentors and other marriage educators. Over the years, 75,000 PREPARE/ENRICH facilitators have been trained in the USA and other countries around the world. A book, entitled *The Couple Checkup* (2008), by David Olson and others, provides a number of exercises to help couples improve their relationship skills.[17] This programme is actively promoted in the UK, and works in partnership with the Marriage Course of Holy Trinity Brompton, London, the home of the Alpha Course.

The Association for Couples in Marriage Enrichment (ACME)

This Association is an international organisation founded in 1973. Its approach is to help married couples develop skills in communication, conflict resolution, and commitment. The programme is presented at weekend retreats and ongoing weekly meetings. ACME's philosophy is to 'have an emphasis on the marriage partners as equals, and their goal is to use that equality to become closer as they walk together.'[18] So the ACME formula is to promote human potential, psychological techniques and total equality for husband and wife.

Marriage Encounter

Marriage Encounter, with its roots in the Roman Catholic Church, is now a worldwide movement which is active in over 80 countries, including the UK and the USA. Weekend programmes are run where married couples can develop, in their own terms, a vision for their relationship.

Before attending a marriage preparation course couples are usually required to complete the FOCCUS (Facilitating Open Couple Communication, Understanding and Study) questionnaire, designed in 1985 by Dr Barbara Markey, an enterprising nun with a doctorate in psychology, and a practising marriage therapist in Omaha. (Not long ago Dr Markey was charged with embezzlement of church funds which she had spent on casino gambling, and sentenced to 3-5 years imprisonment.[19]) Such is its attraction that FOCCUS has crossed denominational boundaries, international borders, and language barriers. A version has been developed for use by Protestant denominations and the questionnaire has been translated into 14 languages.

Practical Application of Intimate Relationship Skills (PAIRS)

The PAIRS programme was developed in the late 1970s by Dr Lori Gordon, a marriage and family therapist. The programme is based on a humanistic model that emphasises the importance of establishing and maintaining a positive self-attitude. It integrates a wide range of theories from psychology and psychotherapy and presents them in an educational format. 'In previous generations successful marriages depended upon duty and role competence [ie: male headship]. Modern marriages require greater interpersonal competence as well as equality between partners in peer relationships.'[20]

The goal of PAIRS is a relationship that both partners can live with joyfully. 'For this to happen, each partner must become able to identify his or her own feelings and needs, and learn to communicate them in such a way that they can get met. This means communicating one's needs and desires without making the other partner feel resentful, smothered, burdened, manipulated, or inadequate. Easily and fully meeting each others' needs is the foundation of intimacy, fulfilment, and happiness.'[21]

It is important for us to recognise the very great distinction between the modern version of marriage, promoted by PAIRS, and marriage that depends 'upon duty and role competence', also known as traditional or biblical marriage. Here we see an example of the word 'marriage' being used to describe two entirely different concepts.

The psychological version of marriage

The marriage education movement has its roots in the human potential movement and the humanistic psychology of Abraham Maslow and Carl Rogers. Because of its deep-seated ideological opposition to the biblical view of marriage, the marriage education movement is striving to replace traditional marriage, defined by Scripture, with a new equal-partner version of marriage, defined by psychological theories. In the UK the term 'couple relationship education' is used to emphasise the fact that marriage and cohabitation are considered to be relationships of equal relevance and moral standing. Effectively the meaning of both marriage and the family have been changed by the marriage education industry. In the eyes of marriage education the quality of relationship is everything, and any sexual relationship that meets our needs, wants and desires, and helps us to achieve inner healing and personal growth is acceptable.

The unrealistic claim of marriage education is that with the right skills and communication techniques, couples are capable of experiencing exciting, loving, fulfilled sexual relationships that meet all their emotional needs. But the problems that occur in all human relationships, according to Scripture, are caused by the sins of the flesh common to all men and women, including: adultery, fornication, hatred, selfish ambitions, dissensions, envy, revelries and things like these *(Galatians 5.19-21)*. The only truly effective solution is a new heart and a life that is being transformed by the indwelling Holy Spirit, not psychological techniques which undermine Christian values and standards.

The biblical view of marriage, described in the next chapter, stands in total opposition to the teaching of the marriage education movement.

9
The Psychological View of Marriage

IN THE PREVIOUS CHAPTER we saw that marriage education, which is based on the principles of humanistic psychology and the human potential movement, emerged largely from the initiatives of Diana Sollee, a marriage and family psychotherapist, who set out to change 'the way the culture thinks about marriage'. The aim was to replace the biblical view of marriage with a new equitable version of marriage, and we saw that a number of Christian organisations played a prominent role in the development of this form of marriage education. In this chapter we take a brief look at Care for the Family, a Christian organisation that has been involved in marriage education for the last two decades, and Focus on the Family. Our main concern, however, will be the Marriage Course developed by Holy Trinity Brompton (the church of the Alpha course), for it is the archetypical 'Christian' marriage education programme in both the UK and the USA. First, however, in order to make a true assessment, we must review what the Bible teaches about marriage.

The biblical view of marriage

The Bible is clear that the institution of marriage is a creation ordinance.

At creation God created man, male and female, and commanded them to be fruitful and multiply and replenish the earth *(Genesis 1.27-28)*. God placed the man in the Garden to dress it and keep it. 'And the Lord God said, It is not good that the man should be alone; I will make him an help meet for him' *(Genesis 2.18, AV)*. The role of the woman, created from the rib of the man, is to help him dress and keep the Garden. And here we see the true biblical view of marriage – husband and wife, symbolically, are to work together to keep the Garden.

God ordains the marriage union with these words: 'Therefore a man shall leave his father and mother and be joined to his wife, and they shall become one flesh' *(Genesis 2.24)*. At marriage a man and his wife are joined together by God in a one-flesh lifelong union – the rib symbolically re-enters the man, as husband and wife (now one-flesh) become a new family. Our Lord said, 'Therefore what God has joined together, let not man separate' *(Matthew 19.6)*. Here we have the true meaning and purpose of marriage – husband and wife, working together, are to develop the world God has created. Therefore, true marriage is always outward-looking, as husband and wife work together to build God's kingdom, to serve the church, and to nurture and discipline the children who are the God-given fruit of their one-flesh union.

According to *Ephesians 5* there is an authority structure for the governance of the family; the husband is given the responsibility of leadership and the wife accepts the authority of her husband and submits willingly to his leadership *(Ephesians 5.22-33; 1 Peter 3.1-7; Colossians 3.18-19; 1 Timothy 2.11-14)*. The relationship between husband and wife is based on the relationship between Christ and the Church. The man is the head of the household as Christ is the head of the Church; he is to love his wife as Christ loves the Church. A husband must put the interests of his wife and family above his own. As Christ gave himself for the Church, so a husband must be prepared to give himself for his wife. By loving and supporting his wife he brings great blessing on the family of which he is the head. The wife submits to her husband in all things, as the Church submits to Christ in all things. And she does so with the right attitude for she respects his God-given role as the head of the family.

According to Scripture *(Titus 2.3-5)* godly women with a sound knowledge of God's Word have an important role to play in marriage education. They are to teach the young women good things about marriage and family life. They are to 'admonish the young women to love their husbands, to love their children, to be discreet, chaste, homemakers, good, obedient to their own husbands, that the word of God may not be blasphemed'. So marriage education is a ministry for older Christian women, as they teach young women the virtues of modesty and chastity, and young wives to love and obey their husbands and to be good homemakers and mothers.

With these basic principles of biblical truth we can address the question: Does Christian marriage education faithfully teach the biblical view of marriage? We shall also consider the alternative premise that it is promoting a psychological view of marriage that is devoid of biblical truth.

The National Couple Support Network

Christian marriage education in the UK is being actively promoted by the National Couple Support Network, a partnership between Care for the Family and the Family Life Department of Holy Trinity Brompton. This network aims to offer marriage preparation education to engaged couples throughout the country. The ambitious plan is to appoint a coordinator in each registration district across the UK who will contact engaged couples through churches and registry offices.[1] Engaged couples will be offered a marriage preparation course, asked to complete a psychological questionnaire, and provided with a link to a support couple who will discuss the issues that emerge from the results of their questionnaires. In this way these two organisations hope to take control of Christian marriage education across the UK.

Care for the Family

Care for the Family is deeply committed to marriage education and, as we have seen above, has joined in partnership with Holy Trinity Brompton. It believes that 'research tells us that marriage is good for us – we're more likely to live longer, and be happier and healthier, if we're married.'[2] This is a significant statement for it shows that Care for the Family has built its beliefs about marriage on research. As a matter of policy, Care for the Family does not quote from Scripture in any of its reports or seminars. It simply regurgitates the advice of the marriage education movement, namely, that to have a good marriage we must learn to communicate properly and 'good communication involves resolving to have no secrets, and being open and willing to share your thoughts, feelings, hopes and dreams with one another.'[3]

Rob Parsons, the head of Care for the Family, presents his version of marriage education in the bestseller, *The Sixty Minute Marriage* (1997). He claims to have spoken to hundreds of thousands of people about marriage in cultures across the world. He believes that 'marriages can be revolutionised by somebody speaking plainly about the traumas which hit many of us, and breaking through the sense of isolation that makes us feel "this is just us".'[4] The book gives no biblical teaching whatsoever; there is no mention that the Bible has much to say about marriage. Instead, Parsons provides advice on the usual issues such as effective communications, surviving conflict, handling past hurts and painful memories, dealing with debt, and sex.

It is immediately apparent to the reader that Parsons believes in the power of stories, not the power of Scripture. His stories are like parables from which he draws 'truths' about marriage and the way people should relate to each other. For example, he tells the story of the couple who boasted that they hadn't had a row for six years. Then on Christmas Eve they argued over the Christmas tree lights. As the row intensified, hurts tumbled out that had lain hidden for years. The couple didn't speak for three days and the wife thought the marriage was at an end. But slowly they started to speak and now they are fine except that they argue every two months. Parsons draws his conclusion. 'Was it a good thing that this couple had never had a row? No. Their problem was that they didn't row enough. Few people enjoy conflict but in itself it is not a bad thing.'[5] This advice, which comes from the wisdom of Rob Parsons, is contrary to Scripture – we are instructed, as far as it depends on us, to live at peace with all *(Romans 12.18)*.

Parsons quotes from Agatha Christie, James Dobson, Mahatma Gandhi, Marc Cohn (American song writer), Paul Tillich (Christian existentialist), George Bernard Shaw, Dr Benjamin Salk (psychologist), Jim Boston (psycho-sexual therapist) and Richard Seltzer (surgeon). But he does not use Scripture, for his view of marriage is built around his stories and his grasp of psychology. Not surprisingly, his advice is trite: 'Listen with your eyes'; 'Don't confuse your partner's need for space with rejection'; 'Give your partner flowers when it's not their birthday'; 'Have a television-free evening occasionally'; 'Hold hands more often'; 'Try not to be completely predictable'; 'Try to laugh together'; 'Revisit some of the places that were favourites when you first met'. His understanding of marriage is devoid of biblical truth. Those who read this book are invited to follow Parsons' trivial advice, and are led to believe that Scripture has nothing to say about marriage.

Care for the Family has produced a marriage education programme, called 21st Century Marriage, comprising a DVD and workbook with eight sessions. It is aimed at newly-weds and those who have been married for many years. The course claims to be full of humour, stories and down-to-earth advice. According to the cover blurb, 'For over 20 years, Rob Parsons has helped thousands of couples build a strong relationship. In this compelling film, he lifts the lid on what can make and break those relationships. An easy-to-use workbook accompanies the DVD.' The eight sessions cover the usual kind of psychological advice, such as knowing we matter, acceptance, a time for love, when the sparks fly, and so on.

Focus on the Family

Focus on the Family is now focusing on marriage education. 'The Essentials of Marriage' is an education programme that provides advice from claimed top relationship experts, all of whom rely on secular psychological ideas, and are clearly committed to the concept of unconditional love. The programme consists of three DVDs, three leader books and three participant guide books. *Who Did You Really Marry?* deals with personality types, communication skills and how to resolve disagreements. *Higher Love* claims to help participants find holiness and happiness. *Handle with Care* deals with emotions, sexuality and finance. A marketing DVD, with banners, posters, invitation cards, door hangers, video clips, sermon starters and PowerPoint slides, is designed to help churches publicise an Essentials of Marriage event. The programme is deeply immersed in psycho-education.

The Marriage Course

The Marriage Course (MC), developed by Rev Nicky Lee and his wife Sila, authors of *The Marriage Book* (2000), has spread across the Christian world and is now in 76 countries, including the USA, and continues to grow at a rapid pace. In the UK, the course is held in a whole range of churches, from New Life charismatic churches, to churches affiliated to the Evangelical Alliance; from mainstream evangelical Anglican churches, like All Souls Langham Place, to independent evangelical churches. The course is even popular among Roman Catholic churches.

To many Christians it seems obvious that the MC must be a good thing for it seeks to support couples in achieving long lasting relationships. Yet even a superficial examination of the resources that are used and recommended by the MC shows that it is heavily influenced by psychological thinking. Moreover, because it is presented in such a user-friendly way, few see the danger of introducing the ideas of secular psychology into the church.

Is the MC Christian? It seems to depend on what the participant would like it to be. Its promoters say, 'While the Marriage Course is based on Christian principles, it is designed for couples with or without a Christian faith.'

Significantly, they make no mention of sin, unfaithfulness, selfishness or the hardness of the human heart, as the cause of marital breakdown. The MC promises to help couples grow closer through commitment, through time together, through greater understanding and through developing good habits.[6] And 'whatever your situation, the practical tools you learn will help improve and strengthen your relationship.' The cost of the course is currently £85 per couple.

The need for psychological counselling

Those who lead the MC are told that they will probably need to refer around one in ten couples for psychological counselling. The Lees offer this advice to course leaders: 'We suggest that you make contact with one or more local counsellors in your area that you can refer couples to. The organisations listed below have accredited counsellors on their books that you can get in touch with. Try to speak with the counsellor(s) to make sure they hold similar views and values to you regarding marriage before referring any couples. We've also included a table which provides additional information on counsellors in the UK, US, Canada, Australia and South Africa.'[7] The course leader is provided with hyperlinks to the

British Association for Counselling and Psychotherapy, the Association of Christian Counsellors and the Council for Psychotherapy. In the London area a leader is provided with a list of ten counselling organisations, which offer professional counselling and psychotherapy, with expertise in work stress, loneliness, low self-esteem, bereavement, emotional distress, depression, sexual and relationship problems.

So the MC refers troubled couples, not to church elders for spiritual guidance, but to psychotherapists. What is disconcerting is that Christian couples invited to attend are not told beforehand of the psychotherapeutic agenda behind the MC, and have no idea that they may end up being referred for psychotherapy.

The MC website provides a hyperlink to Relate, a secular organisation which promotes a view of sexuality that is entirely contrary to the Christian view.

The emotional appeal

Central to the MC is a candle-lit meal to the accompaniment of soft romantic music. An atmosphere is generated that prepares an unsuspecting couple for the forthcoming challenge to their feelings and emotions.

In the first session you are required to fill in a questionnaire that focuses on your emotional needs. Then you are made aware that 'to build a close lifelong marriage relationship we need to give time to each other on a regular basis . . . plan to spend, at the very least, 1-2 hours alone each week to rekindle romance, to have fun and to talk together about your feelings.'[8] The MC puts talking about your feelings top of the agenda. According to the course manual, 'marriage [is] designed to counter aloneness'. The essential part of marriage is to 'nurture one another by meeting emotional needs'. We must therefore be proactive in 'focusing on each other's desires'.[9]

In the second exercise, having completed another psychological questionnaire, you are invited to 'write down your own three desires and give examples of how your husband or wife could meet them for you'. For example, you might desire your partner's approval: 'Tell me when I have done something well at home or at work. Show that you notice when I have made an effort.' You might desire a present: 'Give me a present when I least expect it.'[10] You might want your partner to spend more time with you: 'Sit down with me for 30 minutes each evening to talk about the day.' The outcome of this exercise is that in the coming weeks you will 'concentrate on meeting your husband's or wife's desires rather than criticising him or her for not meeting yours'.[11] This advice is similar to that of the ENRICH programme, which persuaded you to make a wish list of 'three things that you want your partner to do more often'.

To encourage husband and wife to focus on their desires is fraught with spiritual danger, for it can encourage them to become self-centred. Moreover, we all struggle against the lusts of the flesh which war against the soul *(1 Peter 2.11)*. The apostle Paul wrote that 'we all once conducted ourselves in the lusts of our flesh, fulfilling the desires of the flesh and of the mind, and were by nature children of wrath' *(Ephesians 2.3)*. Scripture warns that 'each one is tempted when he is drawn away by his own desires and enticed. Then, when desire has conceived, it gives birth to sin' *(James 1.14-15)*.

The art of communication

The MC is all about communication both during and between sessions.[12] We are told that it is important to talk about our thoughts, feelings and desires.[13] *The Marriage Book* explains, 'Deep communication requires us to be open about our inner selves and to make ourselves vulnerable to each other. If we fail to communicate painful and complex emotions and try to cope on our own, we drift apart. For those of us who feel unable to *recognise*, let alone *talk about*, our feelings, change is possible.'[14] (Their italics.)

The problem is that some people have been taught to hide their feelings. We are assured 'effective communication involves allowing our husband or wife to talk about their feelings'.[15] We are taught the power of listening and the problem of defective listening. Effective listening must be empathetic and reflective. That is, effective listening must 'reflect back the feeling in full'.[16] The effective listening exercise requires the speaker to tell 'the listener about the issue and how they feel about it. The listener listens and then reflects back.'[17] We are reassured that 'this exercise is good practice for all of us both in talking about our emotions and in listening to each other'.[18]

The MC, like positive psychology, places a great emphasis on positive emotions. It is claimed that good feelings are an essential ingredient in the recipe for a marriage that meets our emotional needs. But this is not the way of Scripture, for a believer lives by faith, not by feelings: faith in Christ and obedience to God's Word.

Here we should note that the effective listening technique promoted by the MC is really the same as that taught by the PREP programme and Imago Relationship Therapy, discussed in the previous chapter, and has its roots in Carl Rogers' client-centred psychotherapy.

A biblical view of communication

God has created human beings with the gift of language and therefore the ability to communicate with each other. Yet fallen human nature has seriously compromised our ability to communicate with each other, for our sinful heart *(Jeremiah 17.9)* has great difficulty in communicating in truth and love. As *Proverbs* warns, 'Fervent lips with a wicked heart are like earthenware covered with silver dross. He who hates, disguises it with his lips, and lays up deceit within himself; when he speaks kindly, do not believe him, for there are seven abominations in his heart' *(Proverbs 26.23-25)*. So the communication techniques of psychology are a highly unreliable way of uniting people together.

Godly communication, on the other hand, is truthful and comes from the knowledge of God's Word and a heart that is being transformed by the Spirit of Truth. Its purpose is not to get what it wants emotionally, but to edify, to encourage, to rebuke and to teach sound doctrine that accords with Scripture. Our Lord taught that communication should be straightforward and truthful. Our yes must be yes and our no, no *(Matthew 5.37)*. Our speech should always be gracious and edifying. We know that the tongue, which has the power to cause great evil, must be controlled *(James 3.1-12)*. As members of the church of Christ, we are to speak the truth in love. 'Therefore, putting away lying, "Let each one of you speak truth with his neighbour," for we are members of one another' *(Ephesians 4.25)*.

Christian believers, in the fellowship of the Spirit, are to be like-minded, having the same love, being of one accord, of one mind *(Philippians 2.2)*. Therefore, a Christian husband and wife, because they have the mind and the help of Christ, are able to communicate in a meaningful way. As they seek to live by God's Word, they open the door to genuine fellowship, mutual correction, and godly communication.

They do not need lessons from the world of psychotherapy to know how to speak to each other. And their communication is not based on or dominated by selfish emotional desires.

Generating and resolving conflict

And here we come to the climax of the Marriage Course. You are asked to 'take an area in your marriage where you are not communicating with your partner' – whether through neglect, embarrassment or fear – and follow the effective listening exercise.[19] Because the exercise is designed to generate conflict, you are given this warning: 'Some of you may experience a strong emotional reaction to what your partner is saying. Try to put your own reaction to one side and keep listening and reflecting back what your partner is saying.'[20] There is no allowance for the fact that this process invites one spouse to make the most unfair and ridiculous accusations against the other. A major problem with the MC, as pointed out above, is that it does not recognise the sin and unbelief that resides in the human heart. Moreover, once something is said, it cannot be unsaid.

Couples are encouraged to think about ways in which they have hurt their partner, and to write a list. 'Think back to when you were going out, engagement and early marriage as well as recent times.'[21] And more, 'think about ways in which you have been hurt by your partner. The hurt could have been recent or a long time ago.'[22] Examples might be that your wife felt 'rejected when you went out to the pub the night we got back from our honeymoon' or your husband might feel hurt 'when you didn't say anything special about my promotion'.[23] When partners have finished writing down their emotional hurts they exchange lists and silently read about the ways in which they have hurt their partner. One partner then reflects back 'the reasons for their hurt and the feelings it produced in them'. The other partner does the same and the couple then spends 'some time considering every aspect of their hurt',[24] before they forgive each other and comfort and pray for each other. 'This brings healing to the hurt . . . Pray that your husband/ wife will know freedom from guilt.'[25]

Therapeutic forgiveness

The purpose of this foolish and erroneous exercise is to promote a therapeutic view of forgiveness that is contrary to Scripture, as discussed in chapter 6. Moreover, to encourage us to recall and resurrect past sins is also contrary to Scripture, for believers are instructed to forget those things which are behind and reach forward to those things which are ahead. We have God's promise that he has put our sins behind his back; why then should a couple repeat complaints about sins that God has already forgiven and promised to remember no more?

The Marriage Book quotes the experience of a woman (Jennifer) who followed the course. She had had an unhappy childhood because of her stepfather. She wrote, 'How could I possibly forgive John (the stepfather) for what he had done? I was the child. I was the victim. I haven't seen him since I was fifteen – he wasn't even asking for forgiveness.' The MC enabled her to see clearly that she needed to deal with the issue. So she wrote John a letter, 'forgiving him for the hurt and anguish I had experienced as a child in his care . . . as I posted the letter I knew that I had been set free.'[26] Her stepfather was apparently taken aback by the letter and 'unable to see the damage that he had caused or why he needed her forgiveness. Despite his response, the woman experienced complete freedom from the pain that he had caused her.'

The Marriage Book provides a therapeutic view of forgiveness, asserting: 'Where we have been deeply hurt, we will need to keep on deciding to forgive, even on a daily basis, for the same offence. When we forgive as a conscious act, like Jennifer, the feelings will follow . . . our forgiveness is not to be conditional either upon our parents' understanding of where they have failed us or upon a change of attitude in them.'[27] The following prayer is recommended: 'Lord, thank you for your unconditional love for me and your willingness to forgive me freely. Thank you for the good things my parents gave me. I now bring before you the ways they failed me and ask you to help me to forgive them. My father/mother caused me to feel like this through failing to [name the unmet childhood needs] but I choose to forgive them.'[28]

The aim of therapeutic forgiveness is not reconciliation but to make us feel good. The MC is promoting the false doctrine reviewed earlier of therapeutic forgiveness in the church.

Parents and childhood pain

The MC encourages you to have a realistic view of your parents and to 'recognise childhood needs that were not met during your upbringing and any buried hurt and anger . . . Do not be surprised if you encounter strong feelings as you do this. Give God permission to open your heart and express your feeling to him.'[29] In the misery you experience because of your unmet childhood needs, and your unresolved anger, you and your spouse must grieve together and comfort each other. Then you must forgive your parents, although they probably have no idea what you have in mind. Here we should note that this exercise is totally Freudian in concept (and is similar to the teaching of Imago Relationship Therapy).

The Marriage Book asserts that 'the failure of parents to show unconditional love is likely to leave deep wounds. The key is whether our memories of our childhood are happy or painful. For some, these memories are so painful that amnesia has set in and they cannot easily recall anything of what they felt during their upbringing. As a result of experiences from childhood, we may find that at times we react irrationally towards our partner or another third party. These reactions can be very disturbing for our husband or wife.'[30] The implication is that our irrational behaviour is caused by the way our parents treated us as children, and that we are not responsible for our bad behaviour. Rather, we can blame our parents for not loving us enough, and not meeting our emotional needs. This is a Freudian interpretation of life and smacks of the recovered memory scandal of the 1990s, when children were persuaded by psychotherapists to delve into their unconscious to recover (false) memories of parental abuse, and then accuse their parents. Families were torn apart by false accusations of abuse, and many fathers and some mothers actually went to prison solely on the basis of these false memories. The MC is indulging in a similar practice.

The fifth commandment, that we should honour our father and mother, is disregarded by the MC. Contrary to Scripture we are encouraged to be critical of our parents, even to the point of falsely accusing them and labelling them as failures who did not meet all our childhood needs and wants. This is a conspicuously malicious false doctrine.

The false dogma of God's unconditional love

The solution to your childhood hurt is to 'believe God's unconditional love for you as you are now.'[31] The MC promotes the false dogma of unconditional love, discussed in chapters 4 and 5. The compilers write: 'Dare to believe God's unconditional love for you. As you do, God will gradually replace the pain of unmet childhood needs with a sense of security and comfort.'[32] Apparently the pain caused by unmet childhood needs might be so severe that belief in God's unconditional love is insufficient and *The Marriage Book* offers this advice: 'Those who have been deeply hurt may need the help of an experienced counsellor.'[33] An important aim of the MC is to identify those who have deep-seated emotional pain and refer them for psychotherapy.

Why the Marriage Course fails

Are the messages of the MC consistent with the teachings of Scripture? The answer is clearly no, for the MC is promoting a psychological view of marriage that is devoid of and frequently contrary to biblical teaching. Although a few biblical texts are scattered around the manual, the underlying presuppositions are based on psychological theories, with a large dose of positive psychology.

The central premise is that a Christian couple needs to learn a range of psychological techniques to improve their relationship. This approach denies the sufficiency of Christ and is based on a false understanding of Christian discipleship. The conduct of a Christian couple is not guided by psychological theories but by the exhortations and doctrines of Scripture. We are rooted and built up in Christ, and warned not to let anyone cheat us through philosophy and empty deceit, such as the psychological theories of men. All the fulness of the Godhead dwells in Christ and we are complete in him *(Colossians 2.7-10)*. We are to walk by the Spirit, not by the fleshly wisdom of psychology. To understand the extent of the heresy that is being propagated by the MC we need to remind ourselves of God's plan for marriage, described earlier.

The psychological view of marriage

The MC has replaced the biblical view of marriage with a psychological view of relationships. Theories from humanistic psychology, the human potential movement and positive psychology have built a model for sexual relationships and called it 'marriage'. But this is not marriage as taught in Scripture, but pseudo-marriage, the creation of foolish men. The purpose of this marriage is merely to meet the desires and needs of a couple and help them experience positive feelings. It is an inward looking, self-centred relationship in which husband and wife nurture one another's emotional needs and focus on each other's feelings. It does not recognise the concept of sin, and the need for sanctification, and there is not the slightest suggestion that marital problems come from selfish, sinful behaviour.

No distinction between marriage and cohabitation

A fundamental error of the MC is that it does not make a distinction between the one-flesh union created by biblical marriage, on the one hand, and two unmarried people living together in a sexual relationship, on the other. The definition of marriage provided by the MC – a man and a woman joined together in a relationship of growing interdependence – fails to distinguish between marriage and cohabitation. Because the MC recognises no difference, both married couples and cohabiting couples are invited to attend a course. The frequent use of the word 'partner', rather than husband and wife, blurs the distinction between marriage and cohabitation. Indeed, the MC uses the word 'partner' to describe both married and cohabiting couples.

The truth is that the MC is not teaching about marriage at all (as defined by the Bible), but about sexual relationships (as understood by humanistic psychology). It is engaged in what marriage educators refer to as couple relationship education. While the word marriage is still used, the word has been divested of its true meaning and significance. Here we should remind ourselves that the Smart Marriages Coalition has done the same thing – all sexual relationships, whether married, cohabiting or same-sex, are now described by the word 'marriage'.

The MC ignores the biblical concepts of headship and submission; they are not discussed in the seven sessions of the MC. This means that the essential biblical message about the role of husband and wife, and the governance of the family, as described in Scripture, is disregarded. At this point we see the absolute conflict between two opposing views of marriage – *pseudo-marriage* created by the psychological theories of men and *biblical marriage* revealed by God's eternal Word.

The virtuous wife contrasted with the MC wife

Here we draw a contrast between the picture of the virtuous wife, described in *Proverbs 31*, and the picture of the wife the MC hopes to create. According to *Proverbs* the virtuous wife works from morning to night, willingly working with her hands to provide food for her household. She plants a vineyard, she makes tapestry and linen garments as she watches over the ways of her household. She is never idle, for she rises while it is yet night and her lamp does not go out by night. And she cares for others, extending her hand to the poor and needy. She opens her mouth with wisdom and is kind in all her ways. She fully supports her husband when he sits among the elders of the land. She is good to her husband who praises her as a wife of virtue and value. She has no time or inclination to become obsessed with endless, self-centred emotional needs and desires.

By contrast the emotionally bereft wife of the MC is preoccupied with and filled with inner pain. To feel better she makes a list of the desires she wants her husband to meet. She finds pleasure in daily talking about her feelings. She frequently remembers the ways in which her husband has hurt her feelings. She is filled with these inner hurts and often reminds herself of all the people who have caused her emotional pain. She recalls her parents' weaknesses, and identifies the childhood needs they failed to meet. She digs up supposedly buried anger that she feels towards her parents. She takes time to learn the four steps for healing her childhood pain, and the ten points for resolving conflict. She regularly forgives everybody who upsets her and that makes her feel good. She does her best to replace negative emotions with positive ones for this creates, she hopes, an upward spiral that leads to future positive emotions.

The MC husband is a rather pathetic figure who spends his time talking about his feelings, emotions and inner hurts. He equally spends a great deal of time trying to understand her feelings. Their marriage is based in equality, for he has cast aside all those old-fashioned ideas about being responsible to guide and lead the family.

Heretical teaching

The MC unquestionably teaches a heretical doctrine of marriage. It uses a secular model of marriage education, which it masquerades as Christian, thrusting the notions of humanistic psychology and the human potential movement into the heart of the church. Its heretical teaching has entirely misrepresented the meaning of biblical marriage, and because many churches no longer teach about marriage, their congregations are easy prey to the subtle temptations offered by this psychological model.

Church leaders who would be true to the Gospel of Christ must oppose the heretical doctrine that is being taught by the MC and the marriage education movement. The church should stand against pseudo-marriage and teach without compromise the biblical view.

10
The Folly of Cognitive Therapy

THE LAST TWO DECADES in the UK have seen amazing growth in cognitive therapy (CT) – sometimes referred to as cognitive behavioural therapy (CBT). It is now widely used in the National Health Service (NHS), and recognised as a fast and effective problem-solver and life enhancer.[1] It is the treatment of choice for depression and a wide range of other psychological problems.

Such is the enthusiasm for CT that the British Government has launched a major initiative to train around 3,600 therapists over the next few years in the hope that almost a million patients can receive treatment for depression from the National Health Service. A Labour peer, Richard Layard, has argued that the UK needs to train as many as 10,000 new cognitive therapists to meet the mental health needs of the population. The Department of Health, while acknowledging a great shortage of cognitive therapists, hopes that in time it will become the most widely used talking therapy in the Health Service.

The biblical approach to wise counsel

Talking therapies, of course, are not a new idea. Before we consider the claims of cognitive therapy we need to recognise that throughout recorded history people have given each other advice and counsel when in trouble, much of which has been based in common sense. For example, Moses' father-in-law Jethro, when he realised that it was not good for Moses to be judging the people of Israel from morning to evening, said to him, 'Listen now to my voice; I will give you counsel, and God will be with you' *(Exodus 18.19)*. The counsel of Jethro was that Moses should select able, godly men to help him judge. Moses heeded the wise counsel of his father-in-law and was greatly helped.

The apostle Paul is confident that believers, full of goodness and knowledge, are 'able also to admonish one another' *(Romans 15.14)*. The word 'admonish' means to give earnest advice, to warn, to urge and even to rebuke. Getting alongside others with words of instruction has always been an essential part of the Christian faith. Christian counsel aims to develop character, godliness and a life of faith and service. So believers have a duty to help each other in their spiritual journey. 'Therefore comfort each other,' says Paul, 'and edify one another, just as you also are doing' *(1 Thessalonians 5.11)*. At the heart of Christian fellowship is the idea of looking to the interests of others by providing counsel, guidance and mutual encouragement.

Christians and cognitive therapy

It is now widely held by Christians who follow the *psycho-secular* model of depression that so-called cognitive therapy (CT) offers the best chance of helping depressed believers feel better. In her book, *The Essence of Psychology* (1999), Kirsten Birkett extols its virtues. 'The techniques of cognitive-behavioural therapy – gradually working back up through exposure to the feared situation, identifying irrational or negative thoughts and consciously challenging them – are useful for anyone to learn.'[2] Peter Saunders, General Secretary of the Christian Medical Fellowship, said that 'Christians are often suspicious of psychiatry and are unaware of the value of mental health treatments. CBT for instance, which involves replacing unhelpful, untrue thoughts, that contribute to mental illness, with positive, true thoughts that bring healing, is a very good fit with the biblical view of human beings as comprising body, soul and spirit. It was after all Jesus who said that the truth will set you free.'[3]

Church-based seminars on depression, which are becoming

increasingly popular, make a special point of emphasising the benefits of CT. The writer attended such an event where a Christian psychiatrist recommended a Christian self-help book on cognitive therapy to the congregation (*I'm Not Supposed to Feel Like This* – reviewed later). The authors claim that the approach is 'a proven and effective treatment that is fully compatible with the Christian faith'.[4]

Albert Ellis' version of cognitive therapy

To understand cognitive therapy (CT) we need to go back to its roots. In the 1950s Albert Ellis, an outspoken atheist and opponent of the Christian Gospel, developed a form of CT known as rational emotive behavioural therapy (REBT) which is based on the assumption that irrational beliefs inevitably lead to emotional problems. According to the Albert Ellis Institute, REBT is a pioneering form of cognitive behavioural therapy. 'It is an action-oriented psychotherapy that teaches individuals to examine their own thoughts, beliefs and actions and replace those that are self-defeating with more life-enhancing alternatives.'[5] The therapist seeks to uncover beliefs that lead to emotional distress. Ellis asserts that all Christians 'are distinctly disturbed, since they are obviously rigid, fanatic and dependent individuals'.[6] He claims that 'devout belief, dogmatism, and religiosity distinctly contribute to and in some ways are equal to mental or emotional disturbance'.[7] It follows that the therapist following REBT cannot simply accept his patient's religious beliefs, for they must be attacked and eradicated.[8]

Aaron Beck's version of cognitive therapy

Dr Aaron Beck developed his version of cognitive therapy in the early 1960s as a psychiatrist at the University of Pennsylvania. He initially practised psychoanalysis, but soon became disillusioned when his research showed that it was not effective in treating depression. Beck developed a new approach for dealing with emotional upsets based on the idea that a rational man 'has the key to understanding and solving his psychological disturbance within the scope of his own awareness'. Beck's underlying idea is that distorted thinking affects our feelings and behaviour.[9] He argued that 'the therapist helps a patient to unravel his distortions in thinking and to learn alternative, more realistic ways to formulate his experiences.'[10] By analysing our negative thoughts and helping us to think more positively, the therapist helps us overcome our depressed feelings. Over the past four decades Dr Aaron Beck has earned an international reputation as one of the founders of CT.

From his work with depressed patients he realised that they experienced streams of negative thoughts that seemed to occur spontaneously. He termed these 'automatic thoughts', and decided that they fell into three categories – negative ideas about themselves, the world, and the future. He believed that automatic thoughts just happened as if by reflex. 'The patient made no effort to initiate them and, especially in the more disturbed cases, they were difficult to turn off.'[11] He helped patients to identify and evaluate their thoughts and concluded that by doing so they were able to think more realistically, which led them to feel better emotionally and behave more functionally.[12] Because of his flawed view of man, Beck did not recognise the conscience and its role in generating what he termed 'automatic thoughts'.

Beck acknowledges that people have rules which regulate their lives. He says that a person's rules 'provide the standards by which he judges the efficacy and appropriateness of his actions and evaluates his worth . . . the person uses a kind of mental rule book to guide his actions and evaluate himself and others. He applies the rules in judging whether his own behaviour or that of other people is "right" or "wrong" . . . By drawing on these standards and principles, he instructs himself (or others) how to behave in a given situation.'[13] Beck then argues that when 'these rules are framed in absolute terms, are unrealistic, or are used inappropriately or excessively, they frequently produce maladjustment.'[14] He asserts that absolute rules often make us feel depressed and anxious. To be more useful, rules should be remoulded to make them more elastic. 'The therapist and patient work together to substitute more realistic and adaptive rules.'[15] Beck does not understand that the absolute 'rules' which help a person judge right and wrong, and which he would like to make more elastic, come from God's moral law written in the heart of man. We should remember that a believer's rule for life and godliness are the absolute commandments of God.

Aaron Beck's view of absolute rules is similar to that of Ellis, although perhaps not expressed in such intemperate language. The underlying aim of CT is to remould absolute rules to make them more flexible; to do away with absolute 'oughts', 'musts' and 'shoulds'.

An important function of the cognitive therapist is to discover the core beliefs of their patients. 'These beliefs are often formed in childhood and are deep-seated. And these beliefs pop up in everyday situations in the form of anxious or depressed thoughts that lead to negative feelings and behavioural reactions to situations. When patients see how their reactions, mood and other symptoms can improve once they begin viewing situations in a more realistic light, they gradually begin to chip away at their deep-seated core beliefs.'[16]

In Beck's system there is no place for the God of Scripture, so his therapeutic system is based on a false view of human nature. He repeatedly complains about negative thoughts and negative beliefs that cause unhappiness and need to be corrected, but he has no real understanding of the source and cause of the negative thoughts. He has no understanding that man is a spiritual being, created in the image of God. He does not acknowledge the spiritual dimension of life and he does not recognise fallen human nature, or that the conscience cries out. He does not accept that the heart of man is sinful and that sin has consequences. CT strives for self-improvement, and proclaims a pathway to happiness that comes from within man. As such, it stands in direct opposition to Scripture.

Cognitive therapy and Buddhism

In an article explaining the growth of cognitive therapy, Alexander Linklater (journalist and researcher into the world of psychiatry) and Dr Robert Harland (a psychiatrist at the Maudsley Hospital) point out that in a search for meaning, some supporters of CT are looking to Buddhism. 'As they spread out of the realm of research and development into the wider world, some cognitivists – including the 85-year-old Aaron Beck himself – are keen to give a sense of something deeper at work in the idea. And the place they go for affirmation is, interestingly enough, Buddhism. An idea of "mindfulness" is seen to connect CBT with Buddhist doctrines of acceptance.'[17]

When Aaron Beck met with the Dalai Lama in Göteborg in 2005, he began by reciting the dozen or so main points of similarity between Tibetan Buddhism and CT. Beck says that the Dalai Lama 'appeared to echo what is also the essence of the cognitive approach, namely self-responsibility rather than depending on some external force to inspire ethical standards.'

When the Dalai Lama asked for his view of human nature, Beck responded that he agreed 'that people were intrinsically good but that the core of goodness was so overlaid with layer after layer of "negative thoughts" that one had to remove the layers for the goodness to emerge. He [the Dalai Lama] expressed the belief that positive thinking [focusing on positive and good things] was the way to neutralise the negative in human nature. My position was that the best way to reach this goal was to pinpoint the thinking errors and correct them.'[18]

This encounter between Beck and the Dalai Lama is important for it brings to light much about Beck's beliefs and philosophy of life. First, Beck is at pains to make it clear that his worldview has much in common with Buddhism. Second, he believes in the essential goodness of human nature, although he acknowledges that CT is needed to uncover the goodness that lies hidden beneath the layers of negative thoughts. Third, Beck is clear that he does not depend on some external force, such as the God of Scripture, to inspire ethical standards. In his eyes, destructive behaviour is a cognitive problem (rather than sin) that can be corrected by CT. Clearly, Beck's ideology is fundamentally opposed to a biblical view of human nature and its needs.

The grandmasters of cognitive therapy

In 2000 the two masters of CT met for the first time at the 108th Convention of the American Psychological Association. Albert Ellis, looking straight at Aaron Beck, joked that people loved to steal his ideas. In the discussion that followed it became clear that the two men were at one 'with each other in terms of identifying how belief systems underlie behaviour, and how the "shoulds" and "musts" have underlying roots which can and should be changed through cognitive strategies which are convincingly presented as necessary and accepted by patients, with some anxiety at first, and then with lasting and productive changes in beliefs and consequent behaviour.'[19] Here we should note that the underlying philosophy of Ellis and Beck is the same. Both believed that the role of the therapist is to change the belief system of their clients.

Cognitive therapy in practice

The manual *Mind over Mood* (1995), written by clinical psychologists Greenberger and Padesky, describes how CT works in practice. The manual shows you 'how to improve your life using cognitive therapy – one of the most effective and widely practised forms of psychotherapy. Step-by-step worksheets teach you specific skills that have helped thousands of people conquer depression, panic attacks, anxiety, anger, guilt, shame, low self-esteem . . .' The manual claims to be 'an effective tool to learn practical steps to feel better and make the changes you want'.[20] Cognitive therapists emphasise examination of the thoughts and beliefs connected to our moods, behaviours, physical experiences and to the events in our lives.[21] Therapy teaches us how to change thinking patterns in order to create lasting positive improvements in life.[22] We are helped to construct a thought record in order to identify and alter the thinking and beliefs that contribute to our emotional distress.

Questions to help identify automatic thoughts include, 'What was going on in my mind before I started to feel like this? What does this say about me if it is true? What does this mean about me, my life, my future? What am I afraid might happen?'[23] Examples of thoughts that might be entered in the thought record are as follows: 'I'm always going to feel this way; I'm going crazy; I'm no good; I'll never get over this; I'm out of control; I'm a failure; I'm a loser; I'm having a heart attack; I've been taken advantage of; I'm going to lose everything I've got.'[23] It is not difficult to see that the thought record is an exercise in self-pity. It is all about me and my feelings, my worries, my fears, my life, my future, and why people don't like me.

The book *Cognitive Behavioural Therapy* (2008) describes CT as practised in the UK. The key message is that CT is a psychological technique for making us feel better. 'Do you feel frustrated with how your life is going? . . . Put simply, would you like to feel happier than you do?'

We are told that feeling good isn't something beyond our control. 'It is actually right here, within you, simply because happiness, confidence and feeling good about yourself are emotions not life events . . .'[25] We are promised that 'CBT will help you to recognise some of your styles and patterns of thinking that create unhappiness and distress, and to learn how to counteract these so that you can deal with potentially upsetting situations in a more helpful way.'[26]

CT will help us move towards a healthier outlook on life and become adept at changing our thoughts, attitudes and beliefs for the better. It is educational in that it teaches us to become our own therapist. 'Not only do you feel better, you actually know exactly why you feel better.'[27] A key point is that CT is a therapy of change. 'Whatever you think about yourself and your life right now, however you feel and whatever you are doing, if you are not feeling good about everything then simply, you could do better. CBT will help you achieve that.'[28]

To help you work out your goals you are asked to 'consider what it would be like to wake up tomorrow with everything as you would like it to be and ask yourself – what changes would there be in your life? . . . Imagine that you live in a land where every dream comes true. Use your workbook to write down your wishes, hopes and dreams about yourself and your life.' What follows is a list of my wants, wishes, the things that will make me happy. Those are my goals in life.

Another feature of cognitive therapy is the claim that it can help you overcome your low self-esteem. You are invited to enter the negative thoughts that cause your low self-esteem on to a thought record. 'When you have self-critical thoughts, instead of simply accepting them, challenge them, look for alternatives and create a more balanced view of yourself.' To counter the self-critical thought that you have not done enough to deserve an evening off, your alternative thought is: 'Doing things I enjoy helps me feel better about myself and then I relax and think more positively.'[29] Another self-esteem lifter is to keep a daily 'Positive Event Log', where you write down all the positive things that happen during the day.[30]

It is not difficult to see that CT is the opposite of the Christian life. Christ teaches his disciples to deny themselves and take up their cross and follow him. The teaching of cognitive therapy, in contrast, is that I should place my needs, my hopes and my wants at the centre of life – the self-centred nature of the enterprise is clear. Everything about CT is about making me feel good, making me happy, and helping me to have my way. It is simply another self-help psychotherapeutic method by which the client supposedly achieves self-improvement without Christ.

The 'Christian' version of cognitive therapy
'The Essence of Psychology'

In *The Essence of Psychology* (1999) Dr Kirsten Birkett equates treatment for depression with treatment for a broken leg. 'If a person is suffering from depression, he or she will not be able to feel joyful and everything will seem a burden. These people may well be able to grasp the truths of the Gospel intellectually; but the barrier of the mental illness stops the full enjoyment and living out of those truths. Christianity is not a mental cure . . . However, if our minds are not working properly – if our knowledge is not filtering through correctly to the rest of our beliefs – then our minds need treatment, regardless of how much we "know". Seeking therapy is not self-centred and self-indulgent, any more than going to hospital for a broken leg is. But we don't accuse people of self-indulgence when they seek treatment for a broken leg.'[31]

What kind of treatment is it all right for Christians to seek? Birkett says that CT has a strong reputation. 'It has techniques to change your thoughts and behaviour from wrong (unhelpful) to right (helpful) ones.' She admits that 'what constitutes right thoughts is very subjective, and dependent upon what the therapist considers to be right thoughts.' Scripture, however, teaches that right thoughts are those that conform to the will of God, for God alone declares what is right *(Isaiah 45.19)*.

Birkett also makes the remarkable claim that the things that CT recommends are largely in line with what the Bible teaches although without the theological context.[32] We are being asked to believe that techniques derived from Ellis and Beck are in line with biblical teaching. This is an amazing statement that shows a remarkable lack of spiritual insight.

Birkett points out that most Christians have to some degree absorbed wrong beliefs from the world, which conflict with what the Bible says. 'It may be, however, that your false belief is so deeply entrenched and unrecognised that the regular routine of teaching and Bible reading does not shake it, no matter how good the teaching is. It may be that this false belief has so shaken your confidence and upset your thought patterns that you simply can't identify it and get rid of it on your own. If so, you may be helped by therapy which teaches you specific techniques to find and challenge these wrong beliefs.'[33] Birkett advises that 'going to a specialist psychologist in order to learn these things may be simply a practical decision, and it can help your godliness enormously if it turns out that this kind of block to your learning is at the basis of various problems.'[34]

Here Birkett is suggesting that only a therapist can identify a Christian's deeply entrenched wrong beliefs! In her mind a Christian needs the help of the special 'enlightened' knowledge of the psychologist to correct the 'wrong beliefs from the world, which conflict with what the Bible says'. Surely a Christian with false beliefs needs help, instruction, mutual encouragement and comfort from a brother or sister in Christ. Surely it is the Word of God, which is living and powerful, sharper than a two-edged sword that pierces our soul and spirit and discerns the thoughts and intents of the heart *(Hebrews 4.12)*, that corrects deeply entrenched wrong beliefs, not a psychologist. It is Scripture, not a psychologist, that is 'profitable' for teaching, rebuking, correcting and training in righteousness *(2 Timothy 3.16)*.

Birkett concludes that 'the important thing is for Christians not to be afraid of psychology'. We should learn to appreciate the therapeutical benefits it can offer.[35] She is doing her level best to convince Christians that they need to supplement their faith in Christ with the benefits of psychotherapy. What is so dangerous about this teaching is that it sounds plausible and will mislead many. When the church is so superficial as to think that the Christian life is about having our thoughts remoulded by a psychotherapist, then Birkett's flawed teaching will gain popular support.

'I'm Not Supposed to Feel Like This'

The Christian self-help book *I'm Not Supposed to Feel Like This*, is another example of how CT is being promoted in the church. Written by two Christian psychiatrists and a Baptist pastor, the book received an enthusiastic review in *Evangelicals Now*. The reviewer welcomed the book, and hoped it would be widely read and used. 'It seems to me to be the first book which really succeeds in applying CBT (which stands for Cognitive Behavioural Therapy), but might just as well be called Christian and Biblical Therapy when explained from a Christian standpoint.'[36] The first author, psychiatrist Dr Chris Williams, is an accredited cognitive therapist and immediate past-president of the British Association for Behavioural and Cognitive Psychotherapies.

Together, the authors strenuously argue for the integrating of psychiatric reasoning with Scripture. They 'believe that insights from both the psychiatric profession and the Bible have much to teach about worry, fear and depression, and that both provide valuable resources for those experiencing these common problems'.[37] The book seeks 'to use insights from cognitive therapy in combination with biblical principles to help understand and plan ways of overcoming problems of anxiety and depression. Central to this approach are our beliefs/thoughts.'[38] The authors integrate the approaches of Albert Ellis and Aaron Beck (without actually naming them) with biblical teaching to help solve the problems caused by depression.

Depressive illness

The authors are firm devotees of the *psycho-secular disease* model of depression. They accept that when someone feels very low for more than two weeks they have a depressive illness. Moreover, we should understand that when Christians are depressed they 'may try to block how they feel with unhelpful behaviour'.[39] These behaviours are often extreme – for example, Christians may deliberately turn against their church, and 'they may also turn against God (eg: by seeing him as unloving or rejecting) and stop reading the Bible and praying. They may choose actively to cut themselves off from God by acting in a way that they know is against his will – having an affair, becoming obsessed by pornography, spending money only on themselves, starting to drink excessively, etc.'[40] Here the authors are asserting that because the 'depressed' Christian is ill, he cannot be held responsible for his behaviour. Any thought that a believer who behaves in this way should be rebuked and corrected is not even considered. We are being persuaded to accept that depression trumps all other considerations, so that the person suffering with *psycho-secular depression* can behave as he pleases, even to the point of denying the faith. Other Christians are expected to show sympathy and tolerance. To do otherwise demonstrates a lack of compassion and is likely to aggravate the illness of the 'depressed' Christian.

The authors claim that the church can be part of the problem. 'One of the main motivating factors in writing this book has been the belief that whereas our Christian faith should be a major asset in overcoming depression and anxiety it is not infrequently the case that the way supposed spiritual values are expressed by ourselves and others can unfortunately produce exactly the opposite effect.'[41] The inference is that we must be careful about the way we use the Bible when we are with depressed Christians. Those who promote CT tell us that it is usually okay to use texts about Heaven and God's love, but we should not quote Scriptures that instruct Christians to live a life worthy of the Gospel, or that exhort Christians to rejoice always, or that instruct Christians to be obedient to the commandments of Christ, for to do so is likely to make the depressed Christian feel even more guilty.

False guilt or false repentance?

A real problem for the cognitive therapist is how to deal with guilt caused by sin. An ingenious solution has been to create the psychological concept of false guilt. According to the authors of *I'm Not Supposed to Feel Like This* – 'Psychologists and psychiatrists have found that during periods of anxiety and depression, people may unhelpfully and incorrectly feel guilty about things that are either not their fault, or about which they have already been forgiven by God. As a result, feelings of guilt cause them to feel they are utter failures.'[42] Another problem is that the church can provoke feelings of guilt in depressed Christians. 'Sometimes your church can unwittingly aggravate, or even cause, feelings of false guilt. For example in the preaching of sermons that emphasise the fundamental truths of the Gospel we mentioned earlier, these truths can be distorted by our low mood so that we focus upon aspects such as condemnation; and the forgiveness and love of God are overlooked . . .'[43] So, in the eyes of the therapist, even preaching the Gospel can cause a sense of false guilt in depressed Christians.

But Scripture does not mention false guilt. It is entirely a psychological concept that has emerged from the minds of psychiatrists and cognitive therapists. Scripture teaches that sin causes the human heart to feel guilty. Adam and Eve, when they disobeyed God's command, felt afraid and guilty, so they tried to hide from God because they knew that they had done wrong. King David confessed that his sin caused him to be overwhelmed by guilt *(Psalm 38.3-4)*. When the Gospel is preached the Holy Spirit convicts the human heart of sin, righteousness and judgement, and a guilty sinner understands his need for forgiveness.

Can a Christian really suffer from false guilt? It is possible but uncommon. A Christian may, for example, feel guilty about breaking a wrongly-made vow, but straightforward biblical advice is the cure. Usually a true believer is able to rejoice in the great truth that there is no condemnation to those who are in Christ Jesus *(Romans 8.1)*. God has promised that the blood of Christ cleanses our conscience from dead works to serve the living God *(Hebrews 9.14)*. Therefore we draw near to God with a sincere heart in full assurance of faith, having our hearts sprinkled to cleanse us from a guilty conscience *(Hebrews 10.22)*. We have a great High Priest over the house of God, who not only forgives our sin, but who also cleanses our conscience of those things of which we were once ashamed.

A Christian who understands the Gospel and has truly repented of his sins knows the joy of God's forgiveness. Sometimes a depressed Christian may still feel guilty because he has not truly repented of his sin, and so the problem is false repentance, not false guilt.

We must be clear on this point – false guilt is largely a creation of the psychological world, the purpose of which is to try to soothe a conscience troubled by sin. The cognitive therapist explains away the guilt caused by sin by labelling it as false guilt. The psychological device of false guilt is a wicked device, because it misleads a sinner who needs forgiveness, and it leads a person away from the Cross and the hope of true forgiveness.

Changing core beliefs

The authors of *I'm Not Supposed to Feel Like This* explain that as we grow up we learn a range of helpful and unhelpful rules about how we judge ourselves, other people and the world. 'These central ways of seeing things are called core beliefs.' We are told that we have a range of positive and negative core beliefs, and during times of depression our negative beliefs predominate.[44] For example, someone who has experience of being let down by others 'fears that God or the church will let them down'. Someone who has had an unloving father may have problems with the idea that God can be a loving Father.

Here the authors fail to distinguish between the core beliefs of believers and non-believers. They wrongly assume that the new birth does not change a Christian's core beliefs. The inference is that believers, who are still ruled by negative core beliefs, need cognitive therapy, not God's Word, to transform their beliefs in order to overcome bouts of depression. God has put his law into our minds and written his law on our hearts; God is transforming our lives by the renewing of our minds that we 'may prove what is that good and acceptable and perfect will of God' *(Romans 12.2)*. Scripture encourages us to set our minds on things above, not on earthly things. So a genuine believer does not need the vain, futile philosophy of humanistic cognitive therapy to remould his thinking.

According to the authors, 'cognitive behavioural therapy describes a type of treatment that aims to help you to identify and change the unhelpful thinking styles and behaviours that are often a part of anxiety and depression. It can help you in getting better, and can work alongside your Christian faith.'[45] In the eyes of the cognitive therapist, God's Word is not sufficient – we need the techniques of CT to change our unhelpful styles of thinking and to overcome our problems.

The authors encourage Christians to use a thought investigation worksheet to identify their biases against themselves, their negative slants and their extreme, unhelpful rules. We are told that extreme rules can be identified by the words 'must', 'should', 'ought' or 'got to'.[46] We have already heard Ellis and Beck say that 'shoulds' and 'musts' cause mental illness. What then of the Ten Commandments which uses the phrase 'you shall not' eight times? Scripture is full of 'oughts' and 'musts'. We ought always to pray *(Luke 18.1)*; we ought to obey God rather than men *(Acts 5.29)*; we ought to walk to please God *(1 Thessalonians 4.1)*; we must worship God in spirit and truth *(John 4.24)*.

The fallacy of 'Christian' cognitive therapy

The Christian version of cognitive therapy is essentially the same as that used by secular therapists. The Christian counselling movement uses the common grace argument to justify their use of CT. We are asked to believe that God has used the 'wisdom' of Albert Ellis and Aaron Beck, two men who rejected the Gospel, to construct a psychological therapy for the benefit of all mankind, including Christians. But this is a serious error. Its fallacy is to believe that the self-improvement ideas of Aaron Beck can be integrated into the Christian faith. It is impossible to integrate a system that encourages self-centred thinking with Scripture. It is a fallacy to believe that the fundamental beliefs of a believer should be remoulded, because God has given him a spirit of 'power and of love and of a sound mind' *(2 Timothy 1.7)*. A genuine Christian believer is indwelt by the Spirit of God and his thoughts are moulded by the Word of God.

Can a Christian benefit from cognitive therapy? Do you need a thought record to help set your life goals? The answer to these questions is no, for CT is an unbiblical system that uses cunningly devised fables to deny the sufficiency of Christ. It places self on the throne of the human heart. Its whole purpose is to make a person feel good about himself, with no regard to his spiritual need of salvation. It is anathema to the Christian faith, and churches that embrace CT are encouraging Christians to place their hope in the psychological concept of self-improvement. They are denying the exclusive saving efficacy of the Gospel, and following the way of the world. They are in error because they do not trust in the sufficiency of God's Word.

11
The Modern Gnostics

IN THIS BOOK we have explored the teachings of the counselling movement and summarised the flawed arguments for integrating Scripture and psychology. The secular, even anti-Christian roots from which Christian counselling has emerged are plain for all to see. The origins of the psycho-secular model of depression have been uncovered and we have shown the biblical response to emotional suffering. We have identified the unbiblical thinking behind uncon-ditional love and therapeutic forgiveness. We have seen that marriage psycho-education is a product of the human potential movement.

From the evidence examined in this book it is clear that the church cannot benefit from integrating psychological 'truth' and Scripture, and that Christian counselling is a secular 'intruder' misleading the church. What is deeply troubling is that this intruder has found a welcome in theological colleges around the world. Even conservative, reformed colleges have been seduced by the hollow teachings of the counselling movement, so that counselling courses, steeped in psychological theory, are now a major part of theological training.

Behind Christian counselling is a mindset that longs for more than is found in the Gospel of Christ. Just as the Israelites on their journey to

146 Christ or Therapy?

the Promised Land longed for the flesh-pots of Egypt, so the counselling movement covets the mind-healer status from the world of psychology.

In effect, Christian counsellors are fermenting a rebellion against sound biblical doctrine, for they have brought the teachings of psychotherapy, built on the foundations of Sigmund Freud, Alfred Adler, Abraham Maslow, Carl Rogers and Aaron Beck, into the sanctifying processes of Christ. The result is that today many professing Christians have been made dissatisfied with the simplicity which is in Christ. Not content to walk by faith and prayer, they seek to be guided by the psychological 'insights' offered by the counselling movement.

Psychological therapies have become so well established that for many Christians they are now an accepted part of the faith. Ideas of self-improvement are reinforced by the plethora of self-help books that are, for many, standard Christian reading. Books on healing depression, controlling anxiety, learning how to forgive unconditionally, enhancing self-esteem, resolving conflict and enriching marriage are very widely read. In addition, thousands of Christians are being trained in the principles of counselling, and many churches have a counsellor on their leadership team. It is now commonly accepted that only a trained counsellor is able to help those in the congregation who are having a difficult time.

The counselling industry has been a major influence behind the emergence of this therapeutic gospel – a new gospel based on a false view of God and man. Many evangelical churches that once proclaimed a sound Gospel now see the Gospel of Christ as a mission to enhance the psychological health of believers, saving them from a life of low self-esteem, and helping them feel secure and significant. But the therapeutic gospel is not based on the truth of God's Word. In reality, it has perverted the Gospel of Christ (*Galatians 1.7*).

False teaching

The greatest threat to God's people throughout the ages has come from those who claim to speak in God's name but are false prophets. While pretending to communicate the revealed Truth of God, they speak a deceptive lie and twist the Word of God. The main purpose of the *Letter of Jude* is to warn the church of the danger of false teachers. Faithful believers are to contend earnestly for the faith once for all delivered to the saints, challenging those who secretly slip into the church and lead people away from the true Gospel, turning the grace of God into lawlessness and immorality *(Jude 4)*.

Gnosticism was a dangerous heresy that attacked the early church. It taught that the path to God was by secret knowledge from an enlightened teacher who possessed special knowledge that opened the way to true healing of the soul. The apostle Paul refuted Gnostic teachers who were deceiving the Colossian church with enticing words *(Colossians 2.4)*. The central platform of the Colossian heresy was that true believers need more than Christ. According to theologian William Hendriksen the heretics made this offer to the believers: 'We can help you. Faith in Christ, though fine as far as it goes, is not sufficient, for Christ is not a complete Saviour . . . in addition to believing in Christ you must follow our rules and regulations. If you do this, you will conquer and will attain to maturity, to ultimate happiness and salvation.'[1]

The Gnostics taught that for true healing of the soul a believer needed to combine faith in Christ with the secret knowledge that came from the 'enlightened' ones. Paul countered this heresy by emphasising the sufficiency of Christ, and showing that Christ is the very image of God, the Creator of all things and the head of the Church, in whom are hidden *all* the treasures of wisdom and knowledge. The message of *Colossians* is that a believer is established and *complete* in Christ. The hymn writer explains the sufficiency of Christ with these words:

> *Thou, O Christ, art all I want,*
> *More than all in Thee I find.*

Here we note again the similarity between the Gnostic heresy that threatened the Colossian church and the ministry of the Christian counselling movement that offers believers the 'enlightened' theories of psychology, combined with Scripture, to meet their deepest needs. The evil of the integration model is that it attempts to mix God's Truth with ungodly ideas, but such integration is impossible, for light and darkness cannot mix. It is not difficult to see that the integrationists are virtually modern-day Gnostics seeking to persuade Christian people that they need the special knowledge that comes from psychotherapy to deal with the problems of everyday living.

The apostle John warned of false teachers, whom he called antichrists, who were seducing the church. He knew that 'Gnostic teachers were insisting that the teaching of the apostles was to be supplemented with the "higher knowledge" that the Gnostics claimed to possess.'[2] In this context the apostle says to believers, indwelt by the Holy Spirit, 'you do not need that any one teach you' *(1 John 2.27)*. Scripture warns, 'Do not put your trust in princes, nor in a son of man, in whom there is no help' *(Psalm 146.3)*. It is unthinkable that true believers, who are sons of God and will be like Christ when he appears *(1 John 3.2-3)*, need the 'special knowledge' that comes from secular psychology to be transformed into the image of Christ.

The counselling movement is built on the premise that Christ is not enough and therefore the Christian life needs to be supplemented with the 'enlightened wisdom' that comes from psychological theories. We have seen the Marriage Course teach that Christian couples need 'special' psychological techniques to learn how to communicate, and 'special' psychological techniques for resolving conflict, and 'special' psychotherapy to heal their inner pain from childhood. We have heard Christian counsellors say that we need the 'enlightened wisdom' of the cognitive therapist to overcome depression. The Christian counselling movement is surely comprised of modern-day Gnostics.

The message from Scripture is that false teachers are inevitable; they *will* come in to the church secretly, as angels of light. So they are not obvious, for their purpose is to distort the Gospel of Truth by deceiving Christians.

Yet today, despite numerous Bible warnings, the possibility of false teaching is underestimated by many leaders of the flock. When did the reader last hear a sermon that dealt with the issue? And this is very sad, for we live in a time when false teaching is proliferating in the church, yet the pulpit is largely silent. As a consequence the flock is not warned of the destructive heresies that are being brought into the church with the effect of subverting true doctrine and seriously damaging the lives of Christian people.

Deceived Christians

It would be wrong, of course, to conclude that all involved in the massive counselling industry are false teachers. Undoubtedly many true Christians have been trained in counselling with the best of intentions, and out of a desire to help people suffering from emotional hurts. But they have been deceived by the plausible, skilful writings of the Christian advocates of psychological therapies. Having read this book many will feel uneasy, for the folly of Christian counselling is clear when it is challenged by God's Word.

The story of righteous King Jehoshaphat, who 'sought the God of his father, and walked in His commandments' *(2 Chronicles 17.4)*, has a warning today for believers who throw in their lot with those who oppose biblical concepts. Towards the end of his reign, Jehoshaphat committed a great sin by forming an alliance with apostate Israel, and allowing his son Jehoram to marry Athaliah, the daughter of Ahab the wicked king of Israel. When Jehoshaphat visited King Ahab he was asked to join a campaign against Ramoth Gilead. The good king answered, 'I am as you are, and my people as your people; we will be with you in the war' *(2 Chronicles 18.3)*, thereby joining himself with the wickedness of Ahab, and doing so despite a warning from the prophet Micaiah. The prophet Jehu rebuked the king with the famous words: 'Should you help the wicked and love those who hate the Lord? Therefore the wrath of the Lord is upon you' *(2 Chronicles 19.2)*.

We have seen the deceptive theories and practice that are doing great harm to the church. Christians involved in the counselling industry need to examine their consciences and ask if they are being faithful to Scripture. Do you really believe that biblical pastoral care should be contradicted and distorted by the therapies of atheistic humanists such as Freud, Rogers, Maslow, Ellis and Beck?

Conclusion

Having examined the evidence presented in this book there can be no doubt that the Christian counselling movement is full of teachers who are subverting the doctrine and conduct of the church, and leading vast numbers of people astray. Christian pastors, elders and deacons, and others in positions of leadership, have an obligation before God to watch over the flock and protect them from wrong teaching.

We have affirmed from Scripture that Christians may walk in darkness or may be downcast because of adverse circumstances or severe afflictions. We have acknowledged that a small number of people with mental illness suffer from symptoms of depression that need medical help. But vast numbers are now being persuaded that their 'normal' distresses are serious sicknesses, and redirected from Christ to therapy.

As Christians we know that the God of Scripture is able to supply *all* our needs according to his riches in Christ. He is the Wonderful Counsellor and his grace is sufficient for *all* our needs. He has blessed his people with *every* spiritual blessing in the heavenly places in Christ. He is the God of *all* comfort who comforts us in *all* our tribulation. We can cast *all* our cares on him for he cares for us. Therefore, let us come to the throne of grace with confidence, so that we may obtain mercy and find grace to help us in our time of need *(Hebrews 4.16)*.

Notes

Chapter 1

1　The Association of Christian Counsellors (UK) website, Pastoral Care Foundation Course

2　Albert Ellis, *The Case Against Religion*, American Atheist Press, 1980, p2

3　Ibid. *The Case Against Religion*, p18

4　Fuller Theological Seminary website, Integration in the School of Psychology

5　Tearfund Publications website, Footsteps 21-30, 'Healing for our communities and families' by Gladys Mwiti

6　The Association of Christian Counsellors of Nigeria website, Lessons from the AACC World Conference in Nashville, USA

7　Missionary Care website, 'What Missionaries Ought to Know about Psychological Testing' by Ronald L. Koteskey

8　Fuller Theological Seminary website, news 12/10/09, Fuller Receives Grant for Research of Psychology and Religion in China

9　Care and Counsel International website, Transforming Care for a Hurting World

10　Lausanne World Pulse website, 'Care and Counsel as Mission: Christian Counselling's New Global Look' by Bradford M. Smith, April 2009

Chapter 2

1　Gordon Parker, Is depression over diagnosed? *British Medical Journal*, 18 August 2007, volume 335, p328

2　*Christianity Today*, May (Web-only) 2001, Vol. 45, Gays can change says Columbian University Professor's study

3　American Psychiatric Association website, healthyminds.org, 'Let's talk about depression'

4　National Institute of Mental Health website, Health topics, What causes depression?

5　Jerome Weeks, 'Don't be happy, worry'. Awash in antidepressants, Salon Media website, 29 January 2008

6　Ibid. Is depression over diagnosed?

7　Financial Ties between *DSM-IV* Panel Members and the Pharmaceutical Industry, Lisa Cosgrove et al, University of Massachusetts and Tufts University, Psychother Psychosom 2006; 75:154–160

8　Lisa Cosgrove, Student Pugwash USA website, Mental Health Point/Counterpoint

9　The Bible vs. *DSM-IV* in 'Biblical Reflections on Modern Medicine', Vol. 10, No. 4 (58), editor Dr Ed Payne

10　*Diagnostic and Statistical Manual of Mental Disorders (DSM-VI)*, Fourth edition, text revision, American Psychiatric Association, 2004, p94

11　Ibid. p97

12　Ibid. p102

13　*Evangelicals Now*, 'Notes on dealing with depressive illness', March 1999, Dr Klaus Green and John Benton

14　*Evangelicals Now*, letter, Depression, August 2008

15 *Evangelicals Now*, 'Depression: how churches and GPs can work together', by Dr Mike Davies and Charles H. Whitworth, October 2008
16 Chris Williams, Paul Richards and Ingrid Whitton, *I'm Not Supposed to Feel Like This*, Hodder and Stoughton, 2002, p30
17 Ibid. p210
18 Archibald Hart, *Dark Clouds, Silver Linings*, Focus on the Family Publishing, 1993, back cover
19 Ibid. *Dark Clouds*, p10
20 Frank Minirth and Paul Meier, *Happiness is a Choice*, Fleming H. Revell, 1994, p23
21 Ibid. pp30-31
22 Gary Collins, *Christian Counselling: A comprehensive guide*, W Publishing Group, 1988 Collins, p105
23 James Dobson, *Dr Dobson answers your questions about confident, healthy families*, Kingsway, 1987, p82
24 David Seamands, *Healing for Damaged Emotions*, Authentic Media, edition 2006, p137
25 Ibid. *Healing for Damaged Emotions*, p139
26 Alastair M. Santhouse, consultant in psychological medicine, York Clinic, Guy's Hospital, London, *BMJ* 2008; 337:a2262, 28 October 2008
27 Pfizer, Zoloft Ad, 2003
28 Basic Theology website, An Introduction to the Biological, Psychological, and Spiritual Causes and Treatments of Depression, Causes of Depression
29 American Association of Christian Counsellors website, AACC exclusive, Depression: Self-help
30 Christian Counselling and Educational Services website, Workshop to Help Address Depression by Diane Reynolds, Times staff writer, November 14, 2005
31 Jeffrey Lacasse, Jonathan Leo, 'Serotonin and Depression: A Disconnect between the Advertisements and the Scientific Literature', *PLoS Med* 2(12),

November 8, 2005
32 Psychiatry's 'Chemical Imbalance' Ads Debunked by Researchers, mindfreedom news at intenex.net, November 8, 2005
33 Ibid.
34 Joanna Moncrieff, *The Myth of the Chemical Cure*, Palgrave MacMillan, 2008, p221
35 Ibid. p211

Chapter 3

1 Stuart Burgess, *The Origin of Man*, Day One Publications, 2004, p108
2 Robert Reymond, *A New Systematic Theology of the Christian Faith*, Thomas Nelson Publishers, 2nd edition, 1998, p450
3 Mental health: A Report of the Surgeon General, Dr David Satcher, Overview of Mental Illness, U.S. Department of Health and Human Services, National Institute of Mental Health, 1999
4 Ibid.
5 Ibid.
6 Earl Cooper, *Pain of Mind: A Biblical Perspective of Depression*, Author House, 1996, p98
7 Ibid. p109
8 Matthew Henry Commentary online
9 John Bunyan, *Grace Abounding to the Chief of Sinners*, para. 260, cited from *Fearless Pilgrim* by Faith Cook, Evangelical Press, 2008, p141
10 *Evangelicals Now*, 'Depression: how churches and GPs can work together', by Dr Mike Davies and Charles H. Whitworth, October 2008

Chapter 4

1 Joyce Meyer's 'Health Remedy for Busy People' by Laura J. Bagby, website Christian Broadcasting Network
2 Philip Yancey, *What's so Amazing About Grace?*, Zondervan Publishing House, 1997, p45
3 Rick Warren, God's Antidote to Busyness, Stressbusters – Part 2, PDF article on internet

4   Faithworks website, article, Church needs to tackle debt
5   Steve Chalke, *The Lost Message of Jesus*, Zondervan, 2003, p173
6   The Wittenburg Door website, interview with Steve Chalke, by Becky Garrison, Issue 203, January/ February 2006
7   An Emerging Church Primer by Justin Taylor, article on website 9Marks.org
8   Revolution Church New York website, About Revolution
9   Letter to James Dobson, April 2002, No Longer Silent: Clergy for Justice – Raising a Voice Against Christian Intolerance
10 Options Wimbledon Pregnancy Resource Centre website
11 Dundonald Church website, free-webs, Ministries of Mercy, Options Pregnancy Centre
12 Associated Press, Rick Warren Hosting Church AIDS Summit, 28 November 2007
13 Larry Crabb, *Effective Biblical Counselling*, Zondervan, 1977, p70
14 Selwyn Hughes, *Christ Empowered Living*, UK edition, CWR, 2005, p113
15 Ibid. *Christ Empowered Living*, p111
16 Ibid. *Christ Empowered Living*, p109
17 David Seamands, *Healing for Damaged Emotions*, Authentic Media, edition 2006, p22
18 Dr Charles Stanley, *In Touch Daily Devotional*, 'The Power of Unconditional Love', Friday 16 June, 2006
19 Gary Chapman, *The Five Love Languages*, Singles Edition, Northfield Publishing, back cover, 2009
20 James Dobson, Christianitytoday. com, Loving Focus, Dr James and Shirley Dobson, unconditional love is a decision – one that requires more than the leftovers of their time. Posted 9/12/2008
21 Gary Smalley and John Trent, *The Blessing*, Thomas Nelson, 2004, editorial review on Amazon.com
22 Eric Fromm, 'Father Wasson's Principles of Productive Education', first published in *You are my brother*, Huntingdon, Our Sunday visitor, 1975, pp6-8
23 Harold W Becker, *Unconditional Love – An Unlimited Way of Being*, White Fire Publishing, 2007, p7
24 Ibid. *Unconditional Love*, p7
25 Ibid. *Unconditional Love*, p11
26 Roy Klienwachter, Unconditional Love [Internet]. Version 3. Knol. 18 September 2008
27 Ibid.
28 A view on Buddhism website: Four immeasurables: love, joy, compassion, equanimity
29 Great Lakes Buddhist Vihara website, Growing in Love, Ven. Sativihari (A brief excerpt from the talk given at the Vesak retreat, 2002)
30 Eddie and Debbie Shapiro, *Unconditional Love*, Time Warner, 2004, Wisdom books website
31 Aleister Crowley, Liber AL vel Legis, I:39-40
32 Online Encyclopedia and Dictionary website, Aleister Crowley
33 The Voice of Lucifer website

Chapter 5

1   Larry Crabb, *Effective Biblical Counselling*, Zondervan, 1977, p70

Chapter 6

1   David Seamands, *Healing for Damaged Emotions*, Authentic Media, edition 2006, p22
2   *Daily Telegraph*, 7 March 2006, 'Vicar who can't forgive steps down from pulpit', Richard Savill
3   *Daily Telegraph*, 7 March 2006, 'Brave, but she can't forgive the bombers', Anne Atkins
4   *Daily Telegraph*, 2 December 2005, 'I forgive you, mother tells racist thugs who killed son', Nigel Bunyan
5   *Daily Telegraph*, 25 December 2005, 'Archbishop's Christmas message hails forgiveness'
6   Black Women's Health website, Rev Arly Pryor, The power of forgiveness

7   *Evangelicals Now*, April 2007, John
    Benton, Good Friday Forgiveness
8   Quoted in *Business Week* magazine,
    November 28, 2005
9   The Foundation's Power of Purpose
    website emphasises New Age ideas
10 Sir John Templeton website, The
    Quotable Sir John – On Life and
    Spirituality
11 Vancouver Association of Restorative
    Justice website, Stanford Forgiveness
    Project, *Forgive for Good* online
    course with Dr Luskin
12 Nine Steps to Forgiveness from
    Forgive for Good (Harper Collins,
    2002) by Frederic Luskin, cited from
    newconversations.net/essay luskin
13 Robert Enright and Richard
    Fitzgibbon, *Helping Clients Forgive*,
    American Psychological Association,
    2000, p15
14 Robert D. Enright, *Forgiveness is
    a Choice*, American Psychological
    Association, 2001, inside flap
15 Radical Forgiveness website
16 Radical Forgiveness website, The
    Mission
17 *New York Magazine*, 19 Sep 1994,
    'The Body Shop plays hardball', by
    Ruth Davis
18 The Forgiveness Project website,
    News, Tribute to our founding
    patron Dame Anita Roddick
19 Ibid. Touring Pack 2007/08, The
    F Word: images of forgiveness
20 'True Forgiveness' by Lynn
    Woodland, cited from website light-
    works.com
21 BellaOnline's New Age website,
    Anger and Forgiveness, editor Lauren
    D'Silva
22 Hindu scriptures, From the
    Mahabharata, Vana Parva, Section
    XXVIII, Addressing Draupadi, King
    Yudhishthira
23 Maharishi Ayurveda website, Ten
    Ways for Better Relationships,
    Practise Unconditional Forgiveness

Chapter 7

1   R. T. Kendall, *Total Forgiveness*,
    Hodder & Stoughton, 2001, p7

2   Lewis Smedes, *Forgive and Forget:
    Healing the Hurts We Don't Deserve*,
    HarperCollins Publishers, 1984, back
    cover
3   Lewis Smedes, *The Art of Forgiving:
    When You Need to Forgive and Don't
    Know How*, Ballantine Books, 1996,
    back cover
4   Frank Minirth & Les Carter, *The
    Choosing to Forgive Workbook*,
    Thomas Nelson, 1997, back cover
5   Reported by Scott David Foutz,
    Theology website, Frontline News,
    The Father loves you, Toronto
    Airport Christian Fellowship, 12-14
    May 2005
6   Ibid. *Total Forgiveness*, preface xiii
7   Ibid. p1
8   Ibid. p2
9   Ibid. p4
10 Ibid. p4
11 Ibid. p5
12 Ibid. p6
13 Ibid. p13
14 Ibid. p26
15 Ibid. p32
16 Ibid. p33
17 Ibid. p33
18 Ibid. p36
19 Ibid. p37
20 Ibid. p37
21 James Dobson, Focus on the Family
    website, Dear Friends letter, February
    1997, Special Words for the Home
    with a Heart
22 Frank Minirth and Paul Meier,
    Happiness is a Choice, Fleming H.
    Revell, 1994, p156
23 Dr Stanley M. Giannet, American
    Journal of Biblical Theology, The
    Joseph Novella: A Psychological and
    Literary Analysis, 2002
24 David Seamands, *Healing of
    Memories*, Authentic Classics, 1985,
    pp1-2
25 Ibid. *Healing of Memories*, p61
26 Ibid. *Healing of Memories*, p146
27 Oswald Chambers, *My Utmost for
    His Highest*, note 20th November,
    Christian Art Publishers, 1993

Chapter 8

1   Morton Hunt, 'Help wanted: Divorce Counsellor', *New York Times*, 1 January 1967
2   *The Psychotherapy Networker* – Nov/Dec, 2004: Cover story: The Citizen Therapist: Making a Difference – 5 therapists who dared to take on the wider world, Rob Waters
3   Human potential movement, *Encyclopedia of Psychology*, BNet website, April 6, 2001
4   Richard Hunt, Larry Hof, Rita DeMaria, *Marriage Enrichment*, 1998, Brunnel/Mazel, pp35-36
5   Ibid. p15
6   Ibid. pp42-43
7   Ibid. p42
8   Interview with Diane Sollee, Roundtable on Religion and Social Welfare Policy website
9   Ibid. Diane Sollee
10 The Relationships Foundation, 'Building Strong Foundations – The Case for Couple Relationship Education' (2009), Report by Michael Clark, Rose Lynas and David Percival, p3
11 Ibid. 'Building Strong Foundations', p7
12 Ibid. p16
13 Ibid. p42
14 Howard Markman, Scott Stanley, Susan Blumberg, *Fighting for Your Marriage*, Jossy-Bass, 2001, p2
15 Ibid. p6
16 Harville Hendrix, *Getting the Love you Want*, Simon & Schuster, 2005, Introduction, p27
17 Couple Checkup, Married Discussion Guide, David Olson and Peter Larson, p3
18 Article by Bobbye Wood, Fort Worth, Texas, from March/April 2000 issue of Marriage Enrichment
19 'Protecting the Church against Fraud' by Mike McManus, June 1, 2007, article on VirtueOnline.org
20 PAIRS Foundation website, partici-pant.PAIRS.com/about, What is PAIRS?
21 Website of participant PAIRS.com

Chapter 9

1   Care for the Family, Engage website of National Couple Support Network
2   Care for the Family website, Welcome to marriage matters
3   Care for the Family website, article, Are you just 'twittering' in your marriage?
4   Rob Parsons, *The Sixty Minute Marriage*, Hodder & Stoughton, 1997, p17
5   Ibid. *The Sixty Minute Marriage*, p39
6   The Marriage Course Manual, Nicky and Sila Lee, Alpha International, Reprinted 2007, p10
7   The Marriage Course website, Leader's corner, counselling
8   Ibid. The Marriage Course Manual, p13
9   Ibid. p15
10 Ibid. p22
11 Ibid. p23
12 Ibid. p24
13 Ibid. p25
14 Nicky and Sila Lee, *The Marriage Book*, Alpha International, 2000, reprinted 2009, p62
15 Ibid. The Marriage Course Manual, p29
16 Ibid. p30
17 Ibid. p31
18 Ibid. p31
19 Ibid. pp32-33
20 Ibid. p32
21 Ibid. p55
22 Ibid. p56
23 Ibid. p56
24 Ibid. p57
25 Ibid. p61
26 Ibid. *The Marriage Book*, p255
27 Ibid. p256
28 Ibid. p257
29 Ibid. The Marriage Course Manual, pp69-70
30 Ibid. *The Marriage Book*, p251

31 Ibid. The Marriage Course Manual, p70
32 Ibid. *The Marriage Book*, p257
33 Ibid. p252

Chapter 10

1 Christine Wilding and Aileen Milne, *Cognitive Behavioural Therapy*, Teach yourself (Hodder Headline), 2008, p17
2 Kirsten Birkett, *The Essence of Psychology*, 1999, Matthias Media, pp37-38
3 Christian Medical Fellowship, Press Releases, 14 October 2004, 'Psychiatry and Christian Care Can Work Together'
4 Chris Williams, Paul Richards and Ingrid Whitton, *I'm Not Supposed to Feel Like This*, Hodder and Stoughton, 2002, p2
5 Albert Ellis Institute website
6 Albert Ellis, *The Case Against Religion*, American Atheist Press, 1980, p18
7 Ibid. p23
8 Ibid. p17
9 Aaron Beck, *Cognitive Therapy and the Emotional Disorders*, International University Press, 1976, p20
10 Aaron Beck, *Cognitive Therapy and the Emotional Disorders*, Penguin, first published 1976, reprinted 1991, p3
11 Ibid. p36
12 Beck Institute website, Aaron Beck's Biography
13 Ibid. *Cognitive Therapy*, International University Press, p42
14 Ibid. p246
15 Ibid. p246
16 Beck's Institute Blog, Archive for the 'CT Myths' Category, Dr Judith Beck blogs on CBT for the Huffington Post, July 13th, 2010
17 After Freud, by Alexander Linklater and Dr Robert Harland, Prospect Magazine, Issue 123, June 2006
18 Aaron Beck, 'Reflections on my Public Dialog with the Dalai Lama', The Beck Institute, Cognitive Therapy Today, Volume 10, Issue 2, Fall 2005
19 American Psychological Association, 108th Convention, Washington DC, August 4-8, 2000
20 Dennis Greenberger and Christine Padesky, *Mind over Mood*, The Guildford Press, 1995, back cover.
21 Ibid. p2
22 Ibid. p13
23 Ibid. p51
24 Ibid. pp44-45
25 Christine Wilding and Aileen Milne, *Cognitive Behavioural Therapy*, Teach yourself, 2008, p1
26 Ibid. p2
27 Ibid. p7
28 Ibid. p34
29 Ibid. p210
30 Ibid. p221
31 Kirsten Birkett, *The Essence of Psychology*, 1999, Matthias Media, pp78-79
32 Ibid. p79
33 Ibid. pp80-81
34 Ibid. pp81-82
35 Ibid. p82
36 *Evangelicals Now*, September 2002, book review by Gaius Davies
37 Ibid. *I'm Not Supposed to Feel Like This*, p1
38 Ibid. p30
39 Ibid. p74
40 Ibid. p76
41 Ibid. p85
42 Ibid. p191
43 Ibid. p194
44 Ibid. p15
45 Ibid. p127
46 Ibid. p130

Chapter 11

1 William Hendriksen, *New Testament Commentary*, Baker Books, 12 volume set, 2002, Colossians, p17
2 King James Bible, KJV study Bible, Zondervan, 2002, footnotes, p2557

The Dark Side of Christian Counselling
E. S. Williams
155 pages, paperback, ISBN 978 1 870855 65 5

It is amazing how rapidly the Christian counselling movement has spread through churches in the UK, teaching that hurts and depressions once considered part of normal life are illnesses to be treated. It implies that for 1900 years the Bible has been insufficient for the woes of God's people, or for their sanctification, but that now we have the 'insights' of anti-Christian psychologists to make good the deficit.

In this book medical doctor Ted Williams challenges these claims, giving a clear-cut and interesting overview of the counselling movement.

His survey of the careers and teaching of the giants of secular psychology, the pillars of its 'faith', is unique. Nowhere else are these great names so clearly critiqued from a Christian point of view, and their militant atheism laid bare. Yet these are the heroes of new Christian counselling.

What is Going on in Christian Crisis Pregnancy Counselling?
E. S. Williams
91 pages, paperback, ISBN 978 1 870855 45 7

We hear of very many expectant mothers seeking abortion advice, including girls under sixteen. Dr Ted Williams, a medical doctor of long experience, and a noted specialist in the public health field, shows that Christian counselling centres have adopted a deeply compromised approach which provides non-judgemental advice that leaves in place the option of abortion.

Expectant mothers, including so many girls, should always be helped in a spirit of great compassion, but they must be advised according to the Book of God, and its eternal values.

This book will not only inform and warn, but will focus the aims of pastors and all other Christians when they are called upon to extend help to expectant mothers thinking about abortion.

Faith, Doubts, Trials and Assurance
Peter Masters
139 pages, paperback, ISBN 978 1 870855 50 1

Ongoing faith is essential for answered prayer, effective service, spiritual stability and real communion with God. In this book many questions are answered about faith, such as –

How may we assess the state of our faith?
How can faith be strengthened?
What are the most dangerous doubts?
How should difficult doubts be handled?
What is the biblical attitude to trials?
How can we tell if troubles are intended to chastise or to refine?
What can be done to obtain assurance?
What are the sources of assurance?
Can a believer commit the unpardonable sin?
Exactly how is the Lord's presence felt?

Dr Masters provides answers, with much pastoral advice, drawing on Scripture throughout.

God's Rules for Holiness
Unlocking the Ten Commandments
Peter Masters
139 pages, paperback, ISBN 978 1 870855 37 2

Taken at face value the Ten Commandments are binding on all people, and will guard the way to Heaven, so that evil will never spoil its glory and purity. But the Commandments are far greater than their surface meaning, as this book shows.

They challenge us as Christians on a still wider range of sinful deeds and attitudes. They provide positive virtues as goals. And they give immense help for staying close to the Lord in our walk and worship.

The Commandments are vital for godly living and for greater blessing, but we need to enter into the panoramic view they provide for the standards and goals for redeemed people.

Steps for Guidance in the Journey of Life
Peter Masters
134 pages, paperback, ISBN 978 1 870855 66 2

In recent years the subject of how to find God's guidance has become controversial. Some say that God does not have a specific plan for the lives of his people, but allows us to please ourselves. Others say God's will is known by dreams, visions, and 'words of knowledge'.

By contrast with these sadly unbiblical ideas, this book presents the time-honoured, scriptural view that Christians must seek God's will in all the major decisions of life, such as career, marriage, location, and church. Six essential steps are traced from the Bible, and principles are given on additional practical issues such as possessions and leisure activities; ambition and wealth; joining or leaving a church.

Here is a strong challenge to authentic Christian commitment, with an abundance of pastoral advice.

The Lord's Pattern for Prayer
Peter Masters
118 pages, paperback, ISBN 1 870855 36 1

Subtitled – Studying the lessons and spiritual encouragements in the most famous of prayers. This volume is almost a manual on prayer, providing a real spur to the devotional life. The Lord's own plan and agenda for prayer – carefully amplified – takes us into the presence of the Father, to prove the privileges and power of God's promises to those who pray.

Chapters cover each petition of the Lord's Prayer. Here, too, are sections on remedies for problems in prayer, how to intercede for others, the reasons why God keeps us waiting for answers, and the nature of the prayer of faith.

For other Wakeman titles please see www.wakemantrust.org